Children's Music Workshop

presents

The Recorder Fun Book for Young students

We now offer online virtual recorder lessons using The Recorder Fun Book for Young Students.

Get more information and register online at www.musicfunbooks.com/lessons

With coloring pages and extra bonus songs!

™

www.musicfunbooks.com

Introductory Page

Welcome to the fun and wonderful world of recorder playing. By listenng, singing and playing carefully in class and practicing some at home, you will soon be able to play many famous melodies for your friends, family, and teachers. You may even have the chance to play in a concert!

Holding the Recorder

Left Hand on the Top!
Put your first three fingers on the top three holes on the front of the recorder. Your left thumb plays the hole in the back.

Right Hand on the Bottom!
Put your first three fingers on the next three holes on the front of the recorder. Your right thumb has no hole to cover and is used to steady the recorder while you play.

We don't use our little fingers on either hand to play the notes in this book.

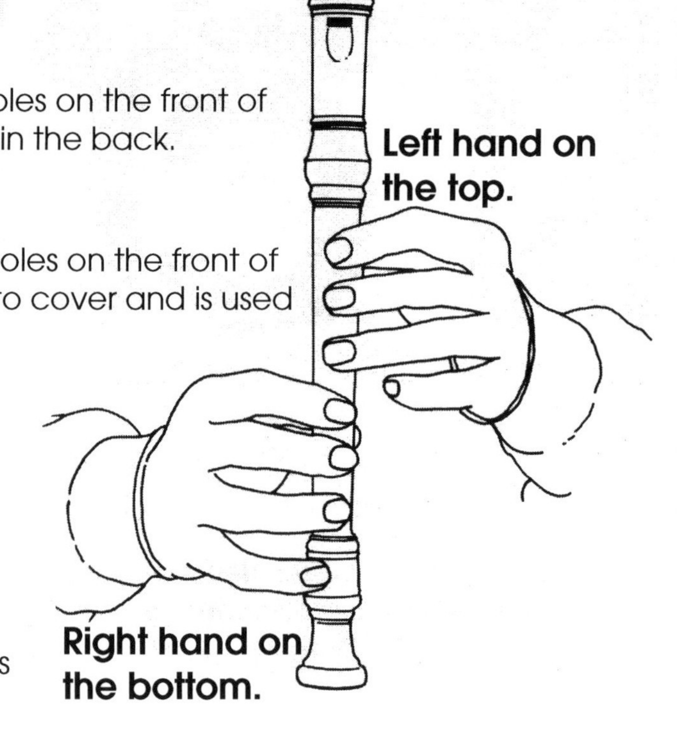

Making a Sound

To make a sound on the recorder, place the mouthpiece on our lower lip. Just a little goes in your mouth - think about softly blowing bubbles with a straw.

Breathe in and very gently blow into your instrument. As you blow, whisper the word "too" very softly. Blow gently. Blowing too hard will cause a high squeak. High squeaks are not allowed in recorder class.

Cover the holes using the fat part - or pad - of your fingers. Don't use the finger tips.

Be careful of leaks. A tiny leak can cause a note to come out wrong or squeaky. Cover up tightly. Check your fingers for round marks that indicate you covered the holes completely. Your teacher will help you find the marks on your fingers.

Warm-Up with Echo Playing

Start each class by holding your instrument with the right hand only a the bottom or bell. Keep your left hand by your side. Listen to your teacher play a rhythm on his or her recorder and then you play it back. Remember all the rules about blowing gently and whispering the word "too". After the warm-up, follow your teacher's instructions and go on with the lesson.

Fingering Chart

Welcome to the wonderful world of recorder playing. Your teacher has shown you how to hold your instrument and make a sound on the mouthpiece. Let's play our first song

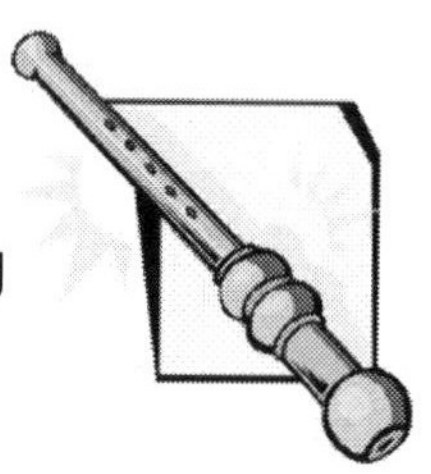

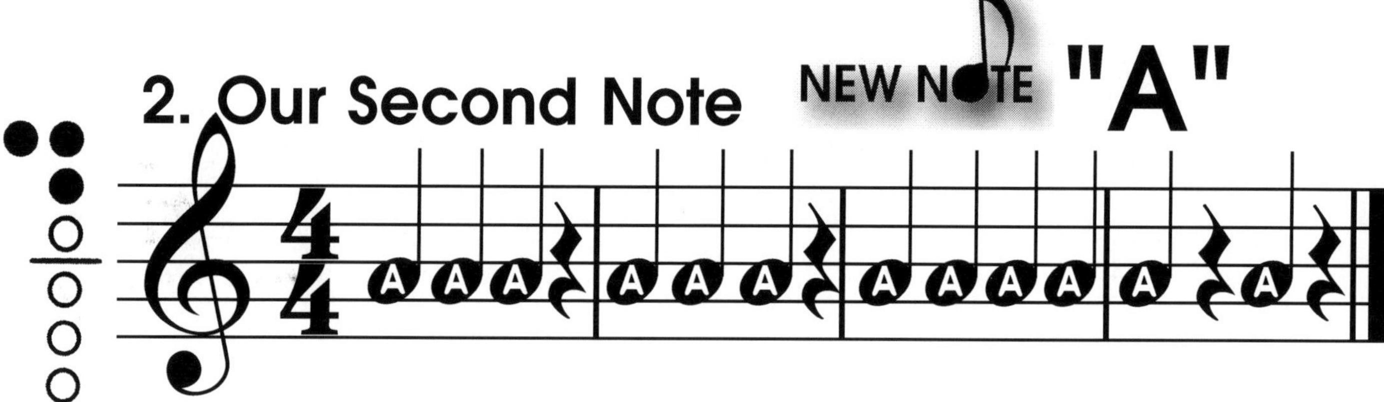

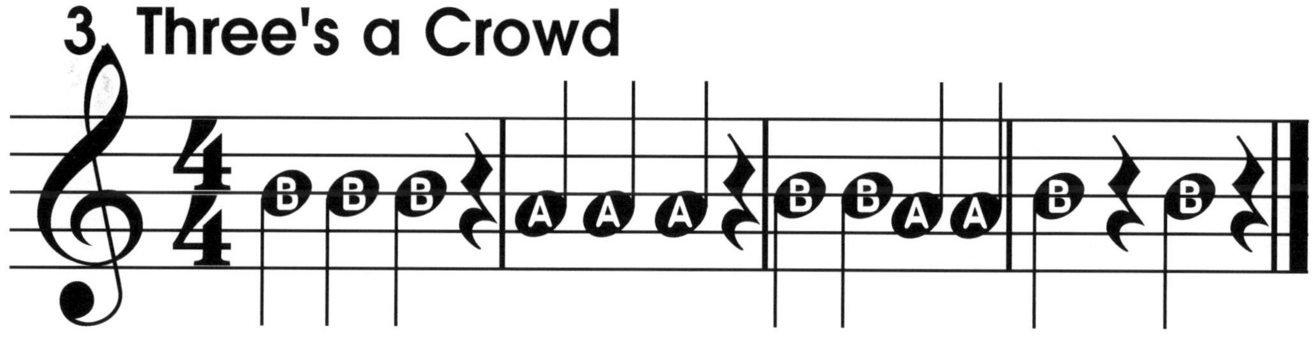

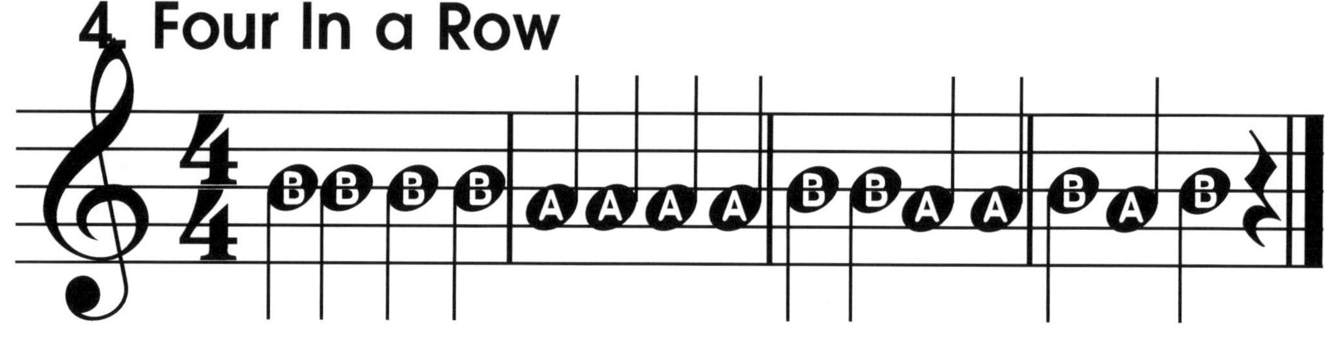

Quarter notes get one beat of sound.

Whole notes get four beats of sound.

5. A Funny Pair

A A | B B |

A A | A B A |

NEW!

Quarter note rests get one beat of silence.

6. Skate Board Sam

A A A | B B B |

B B | A A A |

7. Catch That Note

8. Keep On Blowin'

9. Our Third Note
NEW NOTE
"G"
Cover the wholes tightly. Blow gently.
10. Couch Potato
Whole rests get four beats of silence.
11. Puppy Dogs

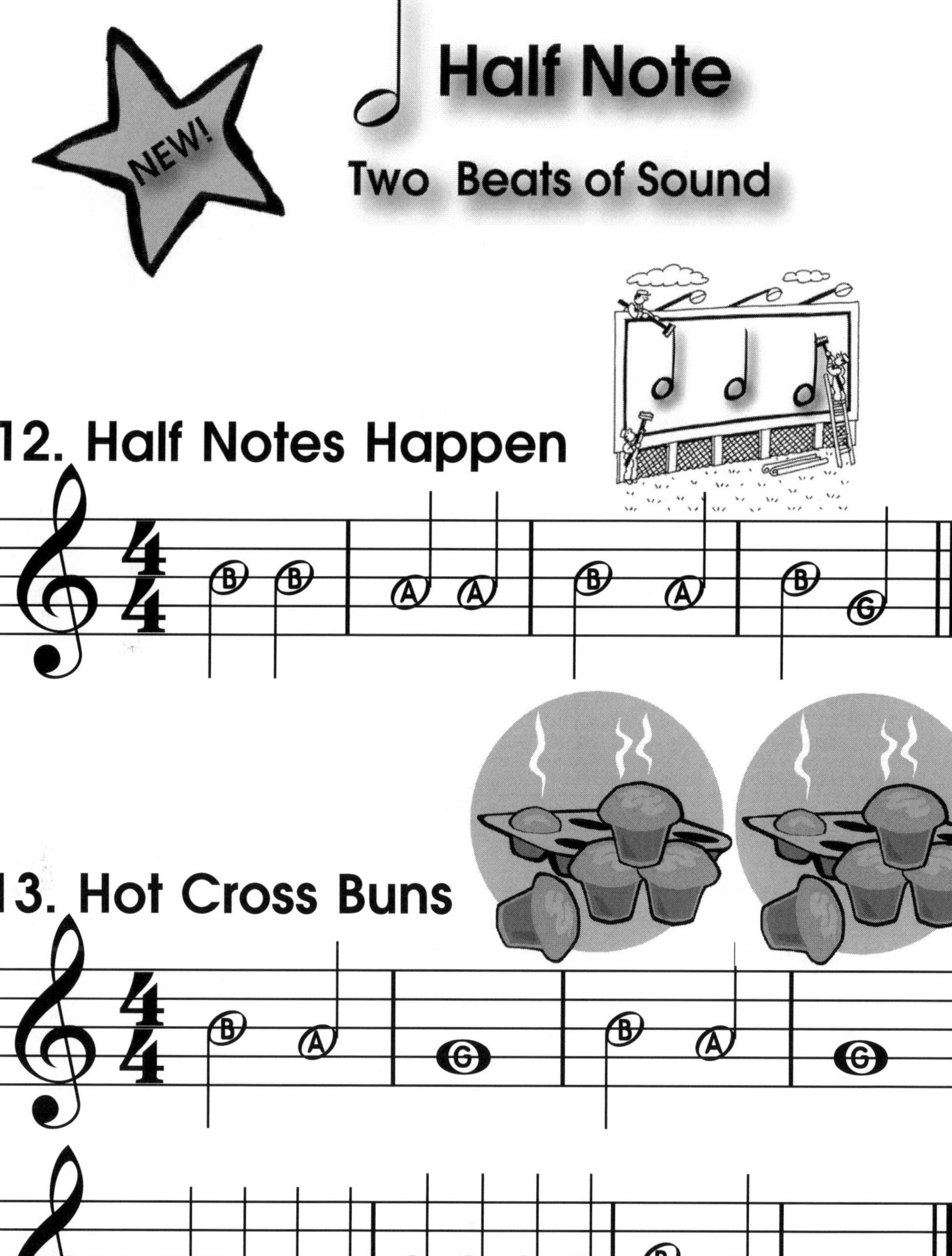
NEW!
Half Note
Two Beats of Sound
12. Half Notes Happen
B
B
A
A
B
A
B
G
13. Hot Cross Buns
B
A
G
B
A
G
G
G
G
G
A
A
A
A
B
A
G

14. Mary Had a Little Lamb

When you see this logo, follow the link for additional songs and exercises online.

www.recorderfunbook/page9

15. Bad News Bears

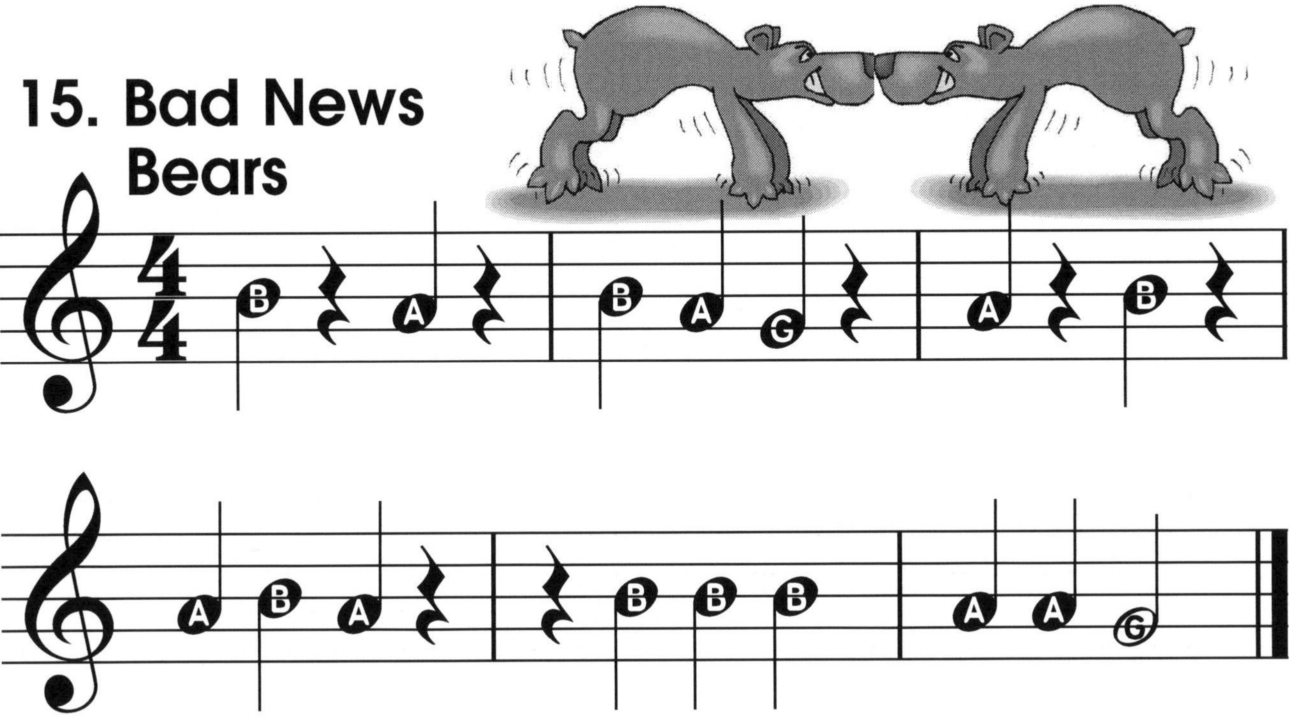

Notes are written on lines and spaces called the "staff".

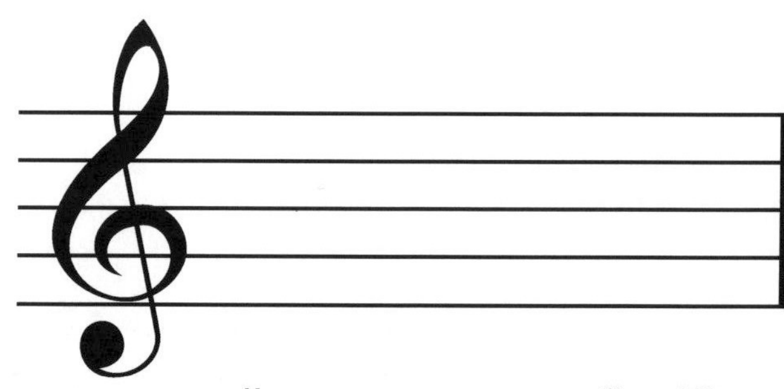

How many lines can you find?

How many spaces can you find?

16. High Dive

17. Our Fourth Note
NEW NOTE
"C"
Keep a good posture. Back straight.
Elbows off your side. Chin up.
18. Apple for the Teacher
C C C C C C C C C C C C C C C C C C C C C C C C C C C C C C C C
C C B B A A G G
C B A A G G

19. Our Fifth Note

NEW NOTE "D"

D D D D D D D D D D D D

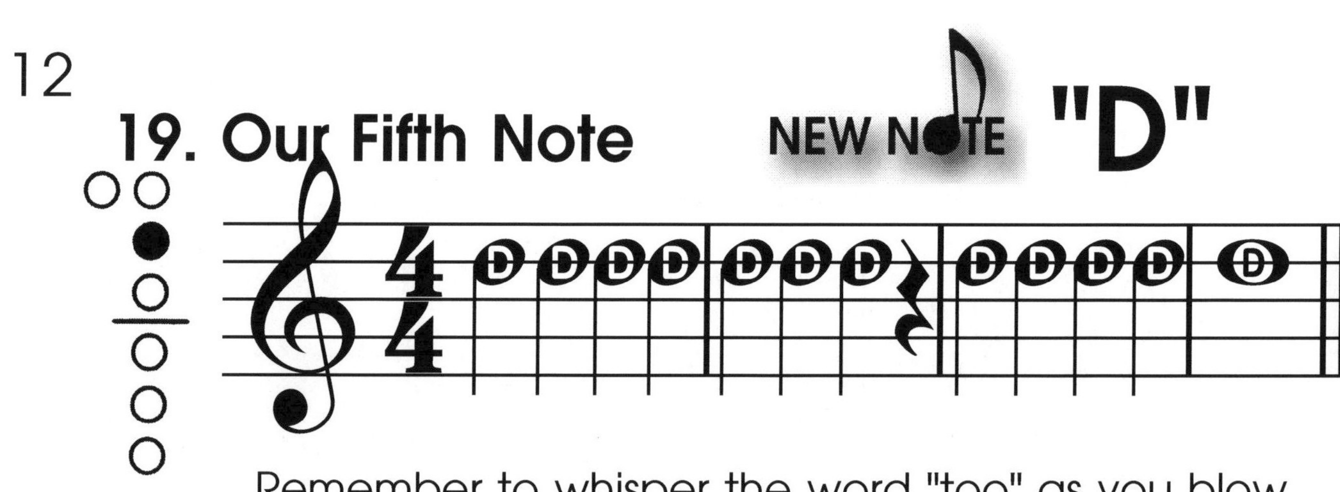

Remember to whisper the word "too" as you blow.

20. Bumper Cars

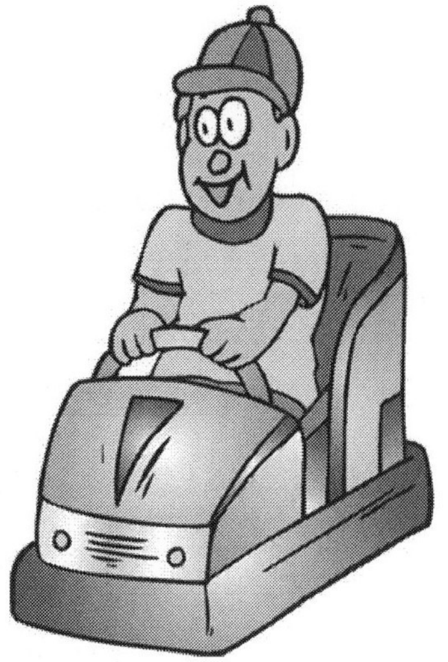

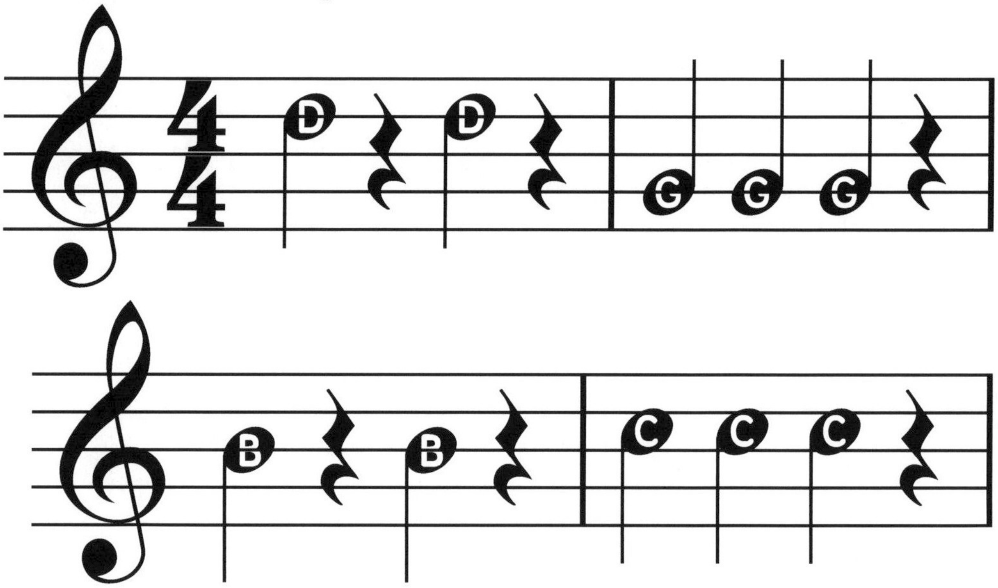

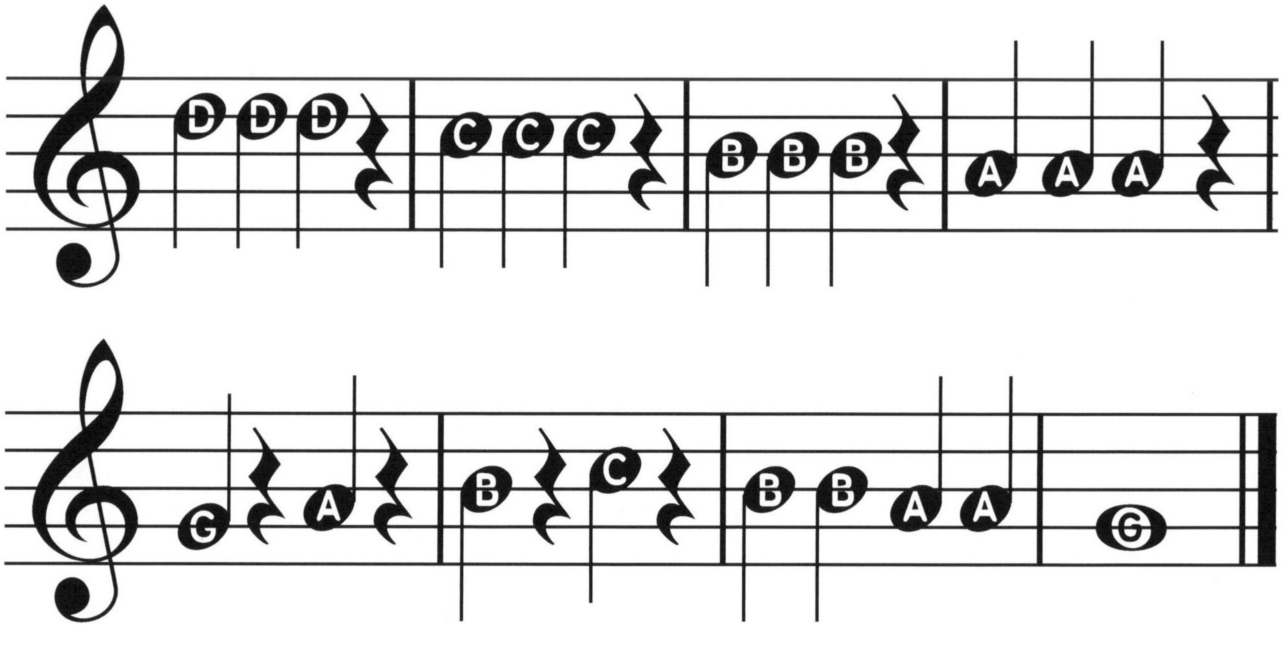

D D G G G
B B C C C

D D D C C C B B B A A A
G A B C B B A A G

21. Dreydl, Dreydl

22. Notes Without Letters

Rhythm Fun

NEW!

Eighth Notes

One eighth note gets 1/2 count.
Two eighth notes get ONE count.

www.recorderfunbook.com/page14

23. Mary's Little Cha Cha

24. French Fries

25. Country Hoe Down

26. Eighth Note Slide
NEW!
A double bar with TWO DOTS at the end of the measure tells you to REPEAT the music.
Repeat Sign
27. The Cabbage Song

www.recorderfunbook.com/page 17

28. Jingle Bells

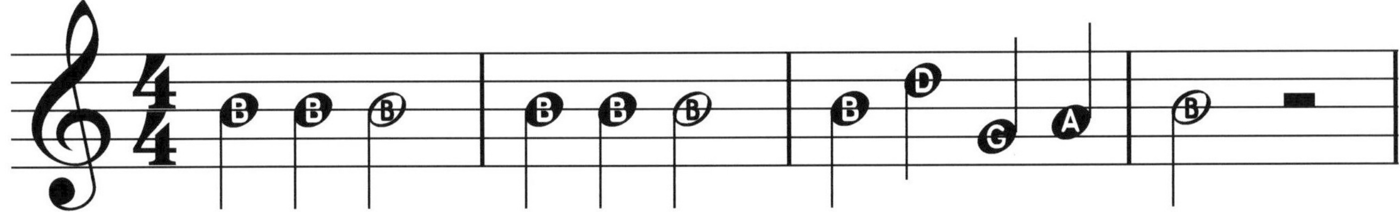

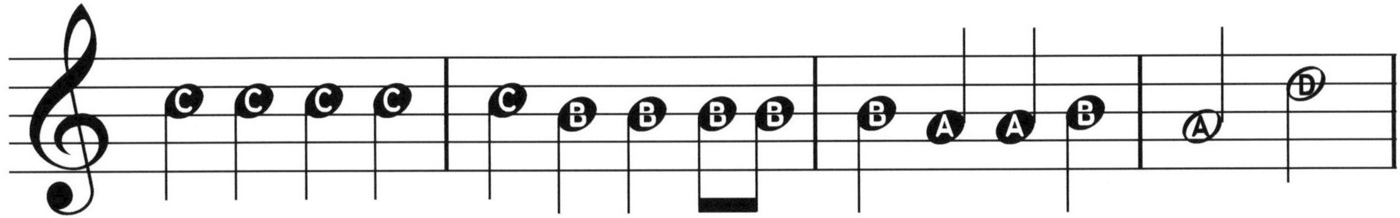

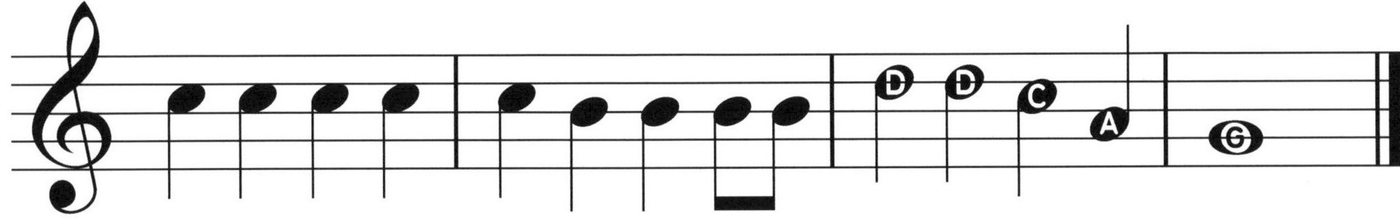

NEW!
NEW NOTE
"Low E"
29. The Karate Chop
30. Rain, Rain, Go Away!

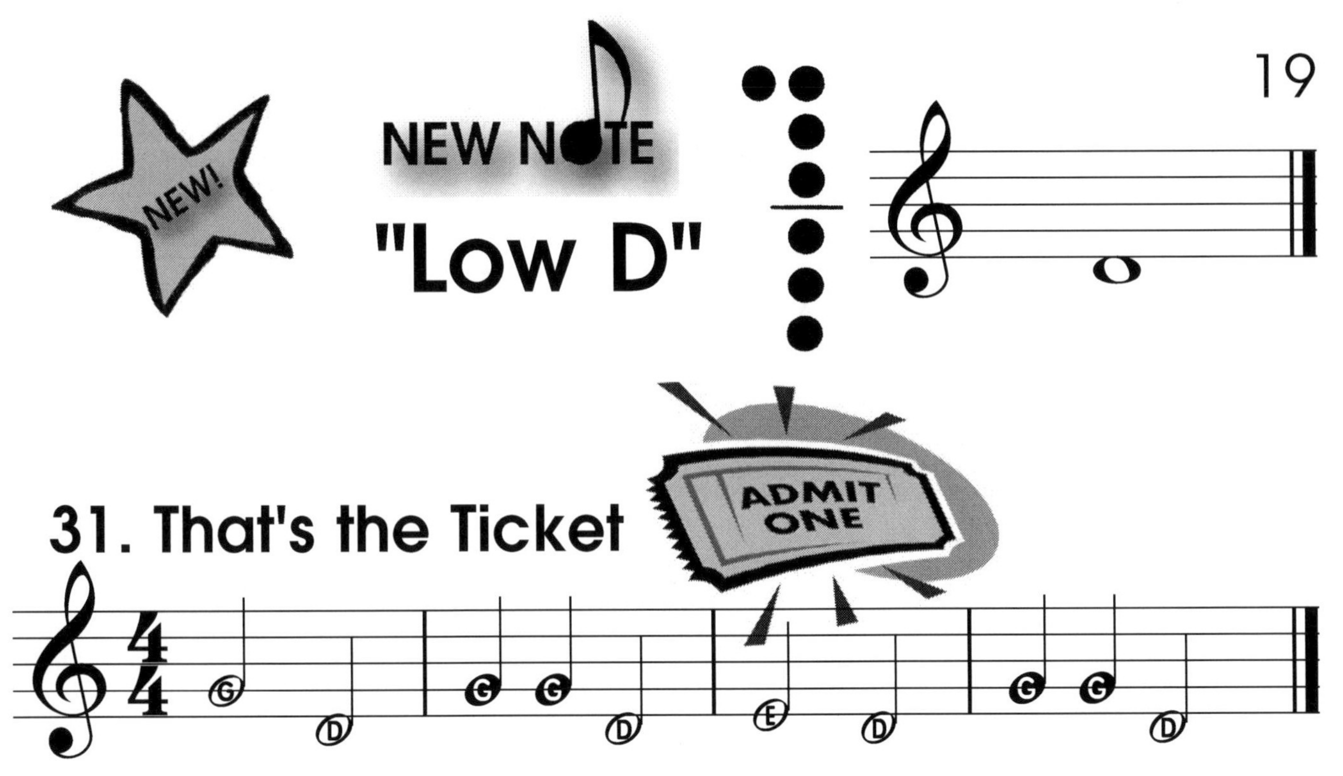
NEW!
NEW NOTE
"Low D"
ADMIT ONE
31. That's the Ticket
G D G G D E D G G D

32. Slam Dunk

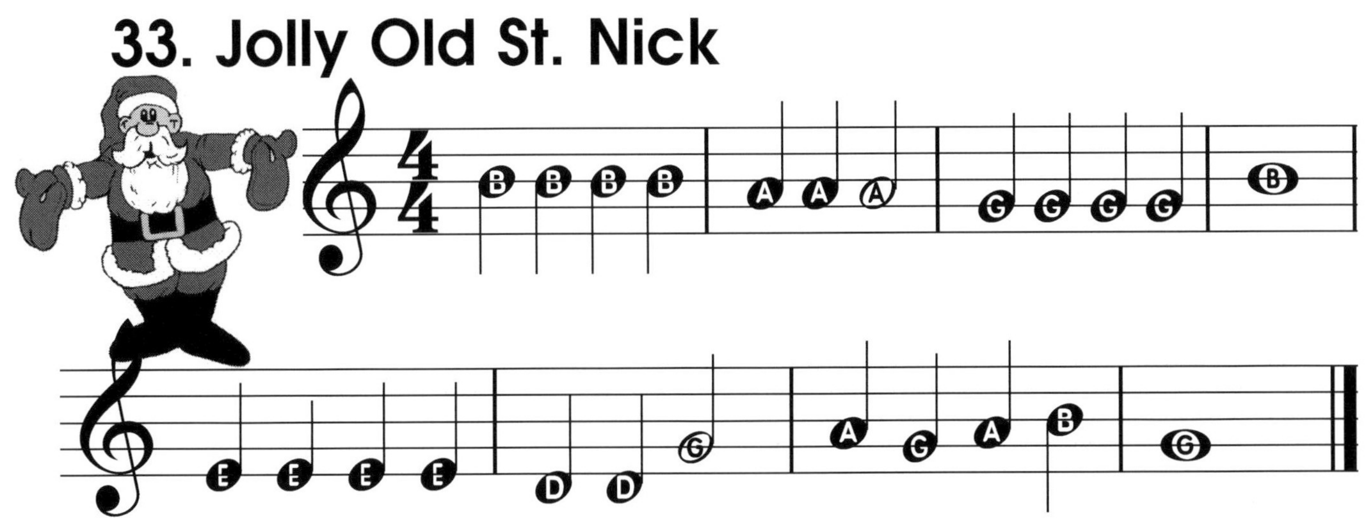
33. Jolly Old St. Nick
B B B B A A A G G G G B
E E E E D D G A G A B G

34. Old McDonald Had a Farm

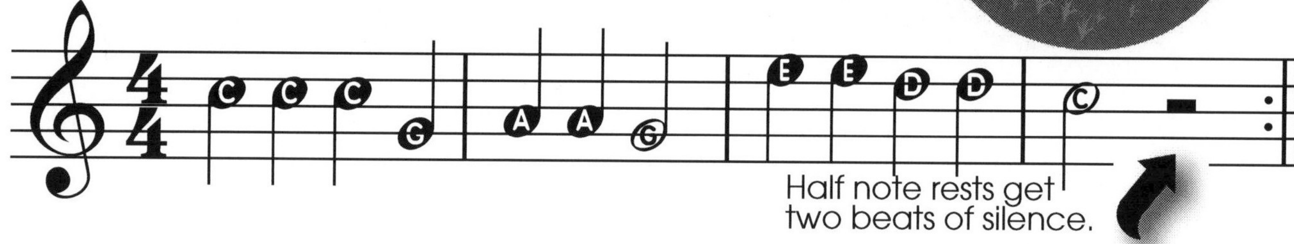

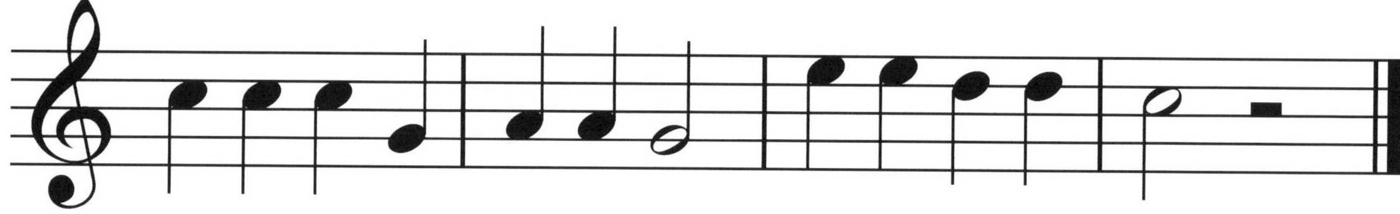

NEW!
D.C. al Fine
Go back to the beginning and play until "Fine".
35. Twinkle, Twinkle, Little Star
Fine
D. C. al Fine
NEW!
D.S. al Fine
Go back to the sign and play until "Fine".
The "sign"
36. Ode to Joy
Fine
D.S.al Fine

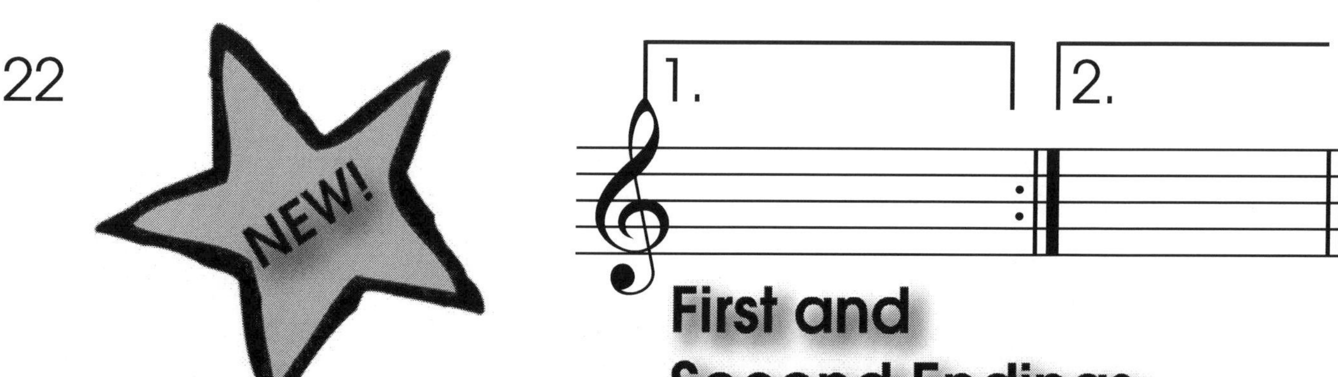

First and Second Endings

When you reach the repeat sign under the first ending, stop and go back to the beginning. When you get to the first ending agair skip it and go to the second ending.

37. Stodola Pumpa

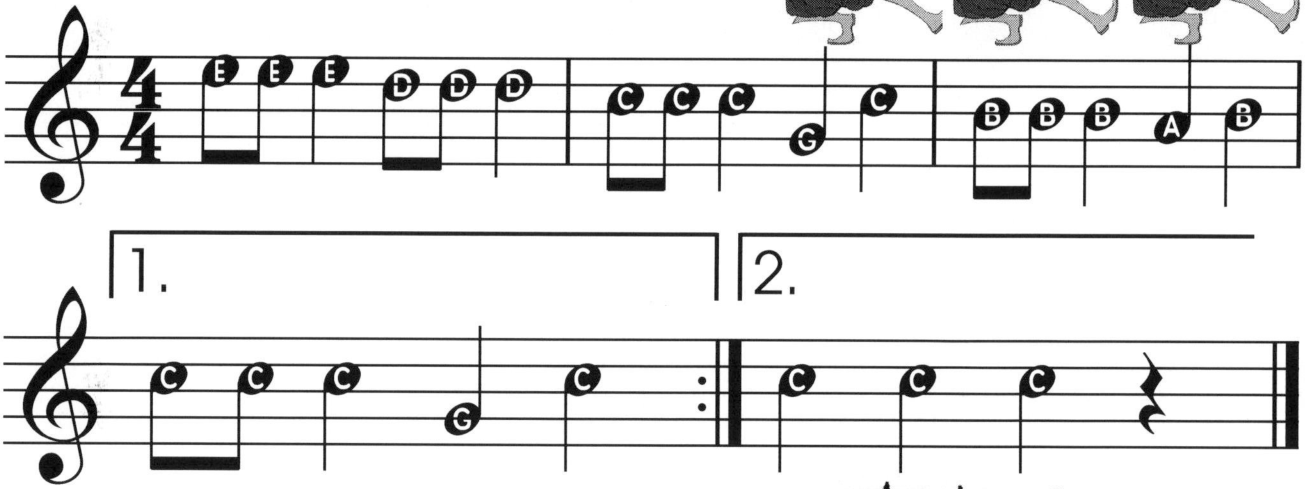

E E E D D D C C C G C B B B A B

1. C C C G C

2. C C C

38. London Bridge

D E D C B C D A B C B C D

A D B G

Slur

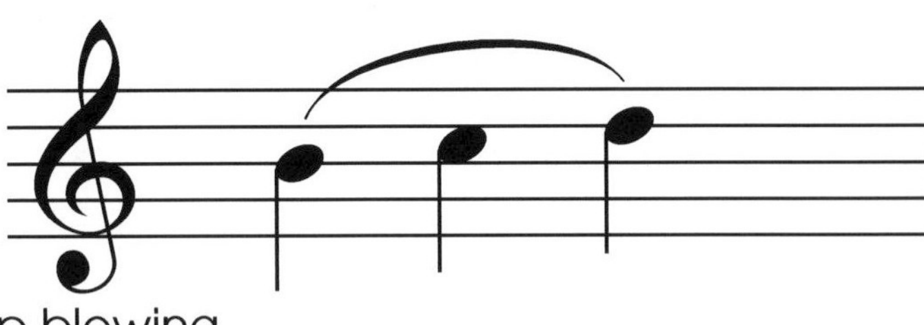

A "slur" is a curved line that connects two or more notes of different pitches. Tongue the first note and move to the next notes without tonguing. Don't stop blowing.

Tie

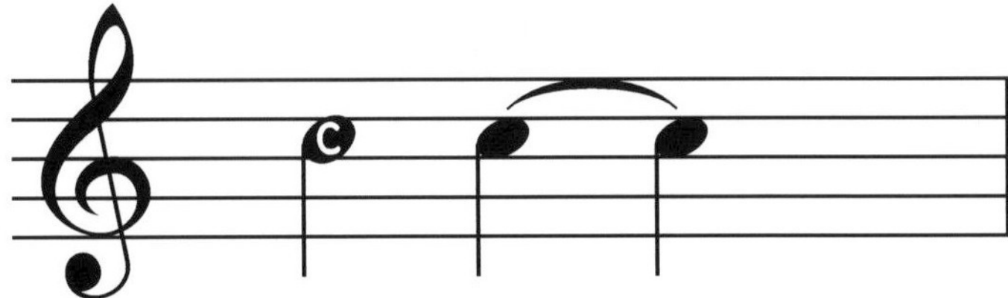

A "tie" is a curved line that connects two or more notes of the same pitch. Hold the note for the combined value of the notes.

Dotted Half Note

A dotted half note gets three beats of sound.

39. Southern Roses

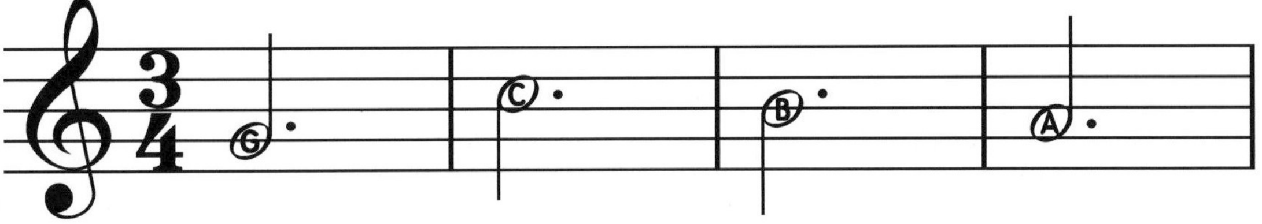

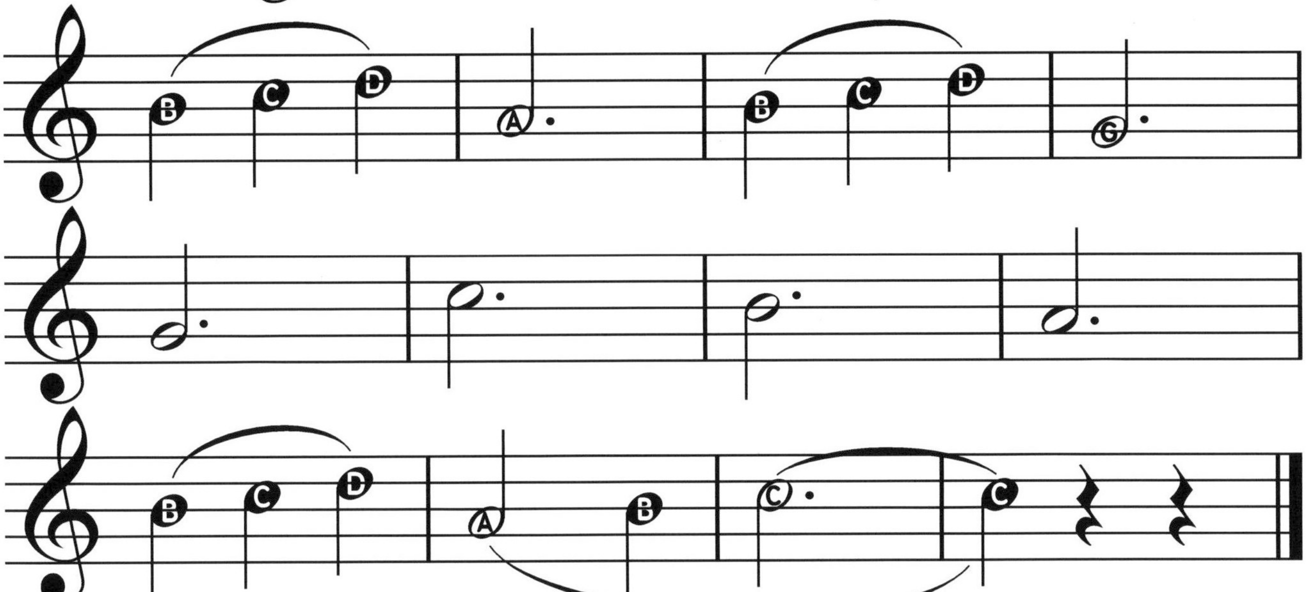

Pick-Up Notes

Note(s) that come before the first full measure of a piece of music.

Fermata (Hold)

Hold (keep blowing) the note until your director tells you to stop.

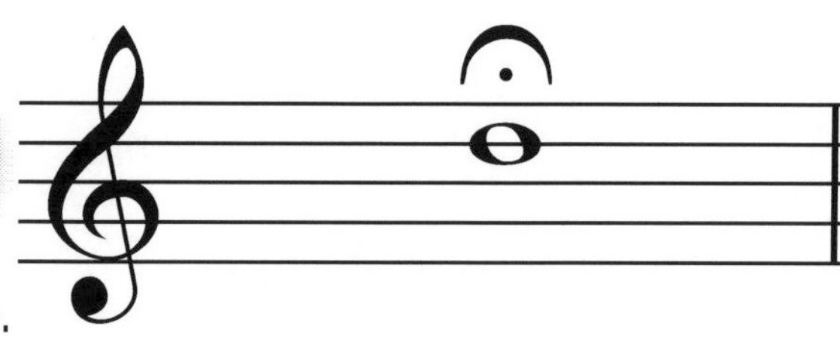

40. Snake Charmer

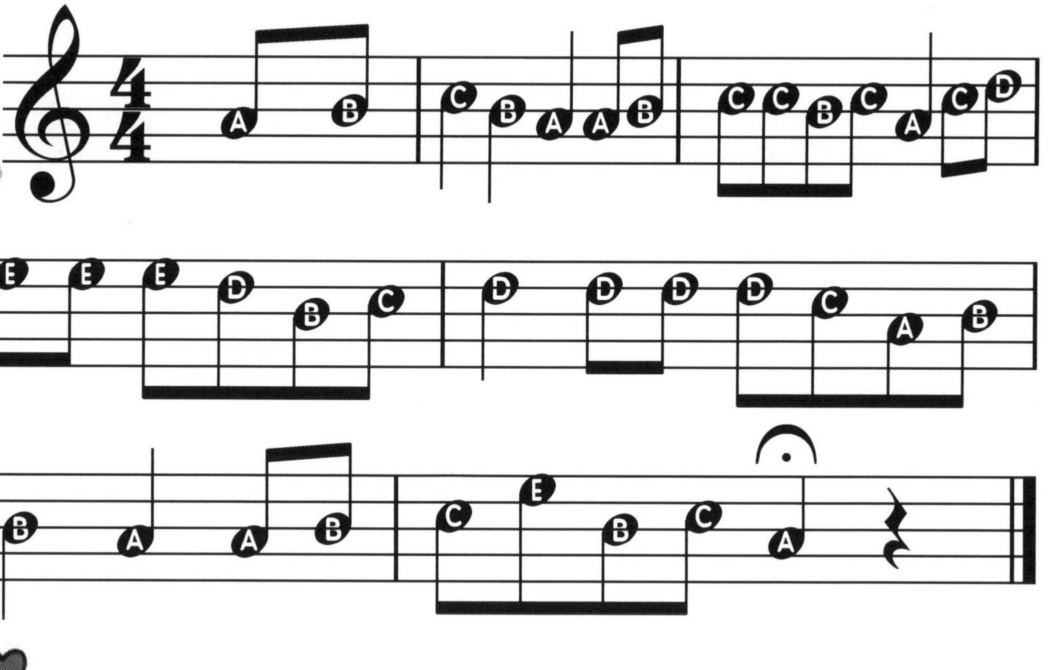

A B C B A A B C C B C A C D E E E E D B C D D D D C A B C B A A B C E B C A

41. Aura Lee

G C B C D A D C B A B C G

NEW!

NEW NOTE

"F#"

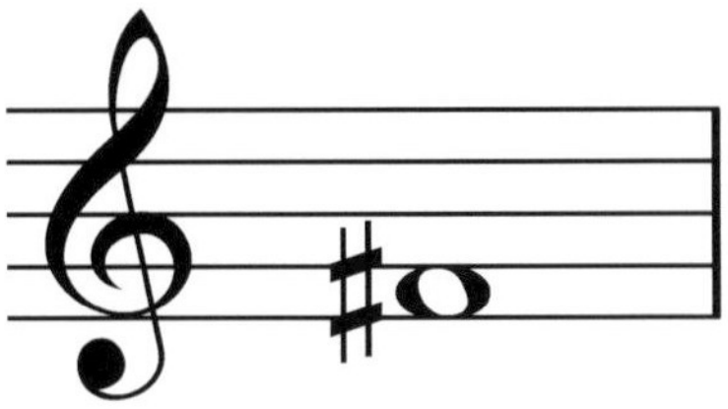

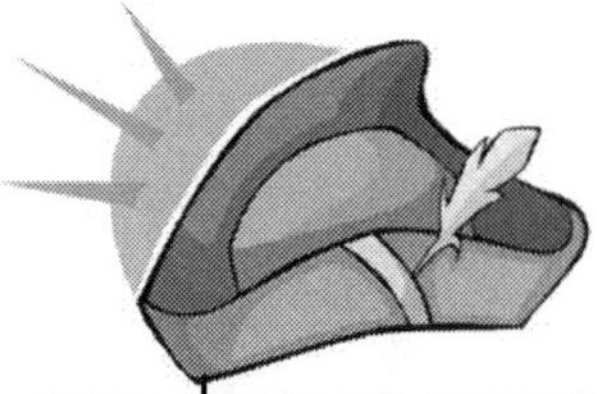

42. Yankee Doodle

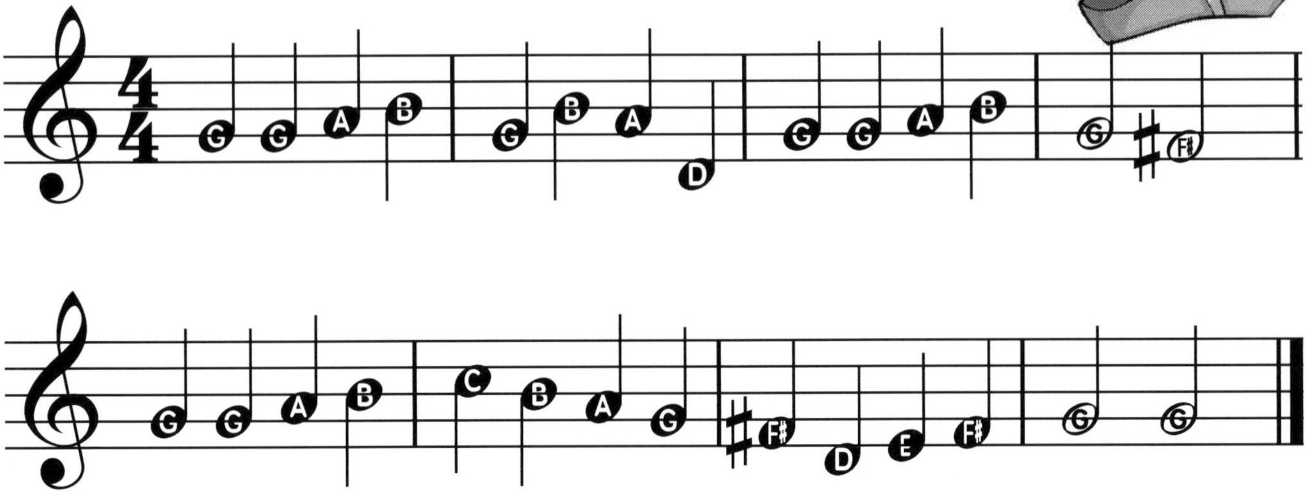

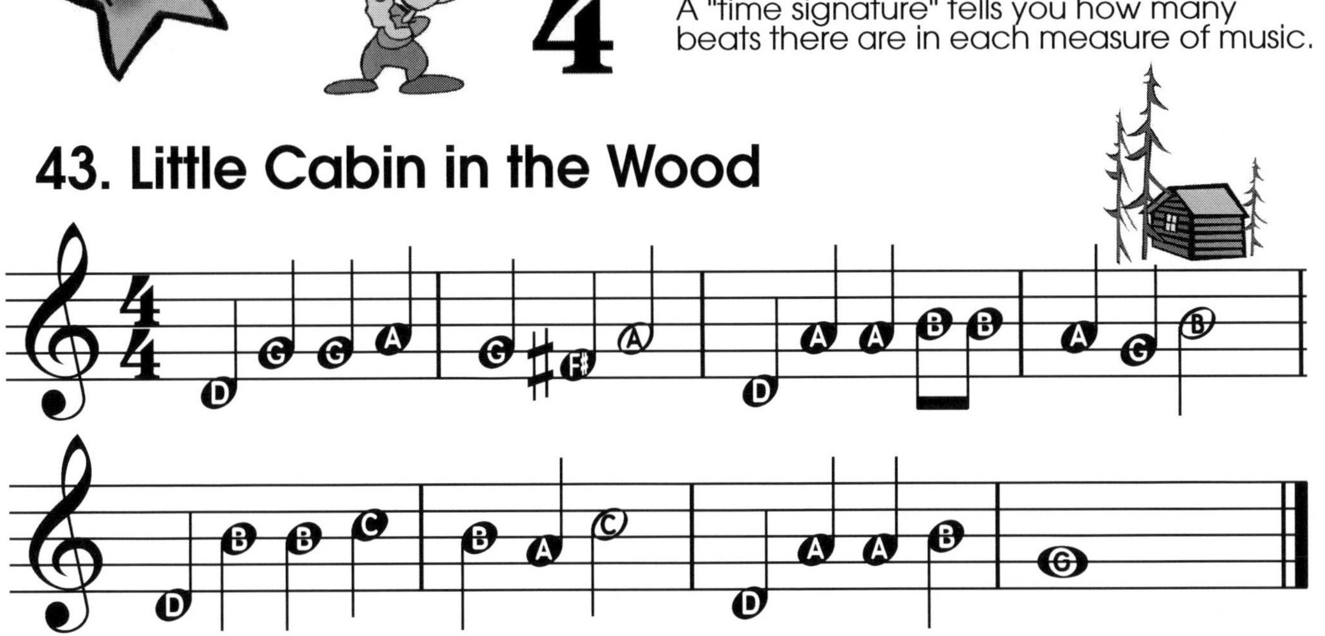

Time Signature

A "time signature" tells you how many beats there are in each measure of music.

43. Little Cabin in the Wood

NEW!

Key Signature

A "key signature" changes certain notes throughout a piece of music.

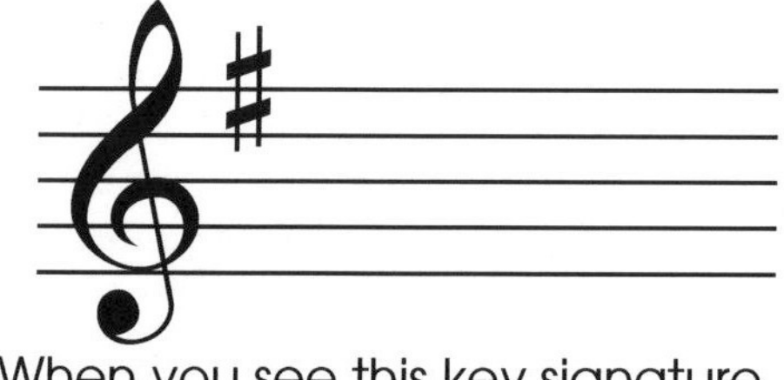

When you see this key signature, play all the Fs as F SHARP.

44. It's a Ringer!

www.recorderfunbook.com/page26

45. Polly Wolly Doodle

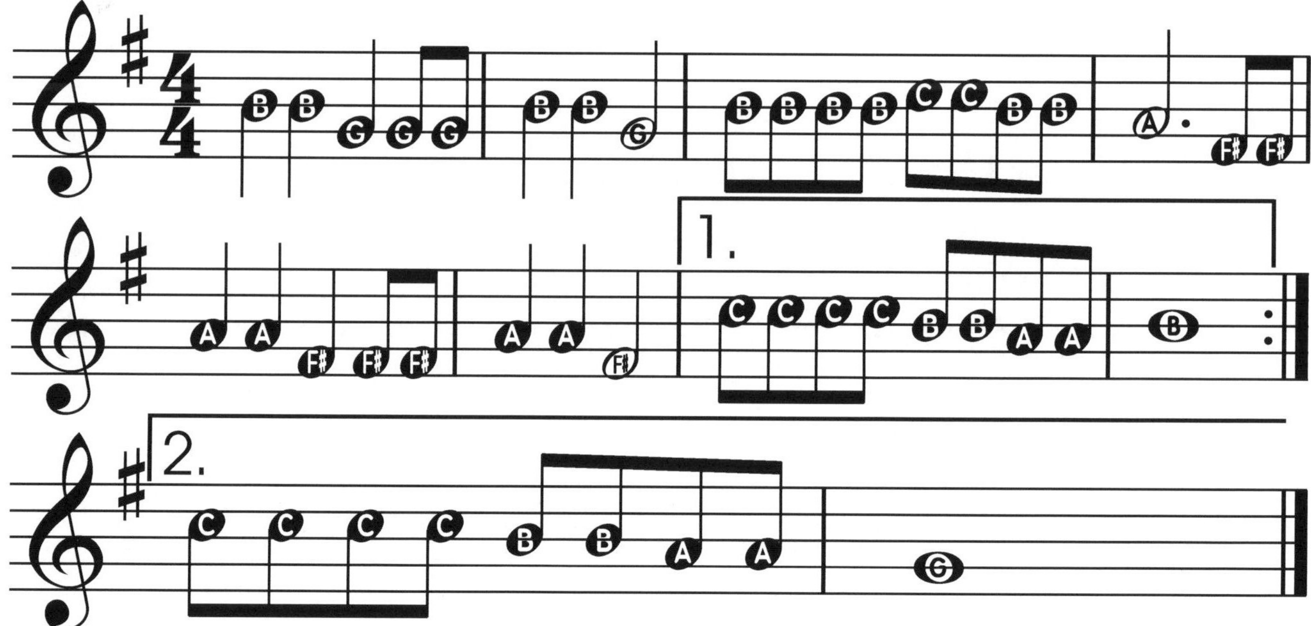

46. Barcarolle

www.recorderfunbook.com/page27

Fun Work

Write in the letters to these notes.

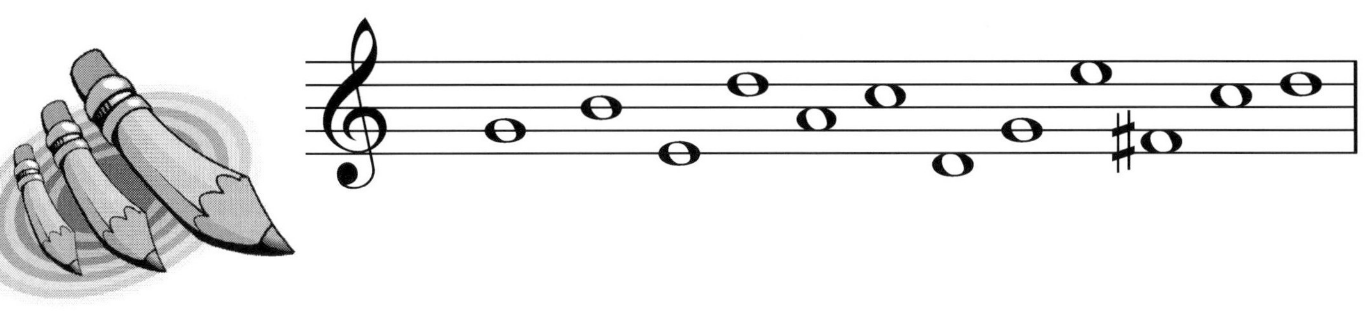

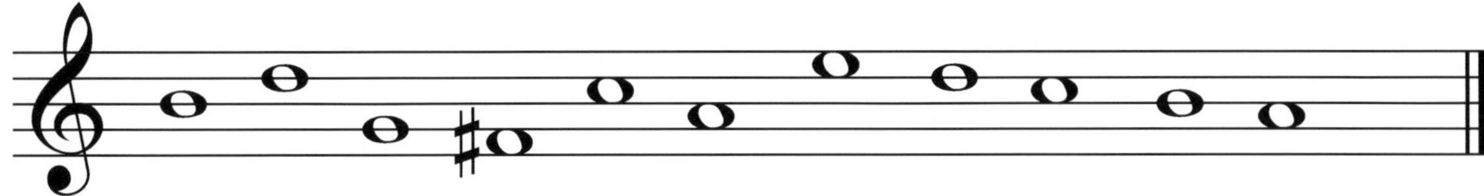

Duet

Two performers or singers who play together.

47. Lightly Row (Part 1 - Melody)

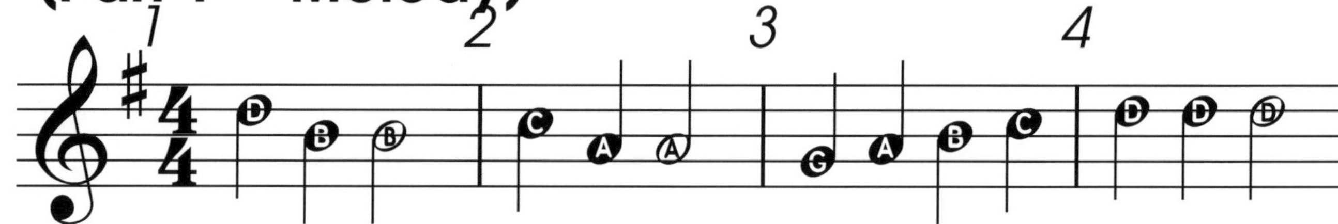

48. Lightly Row (Part 2 - Harmony)

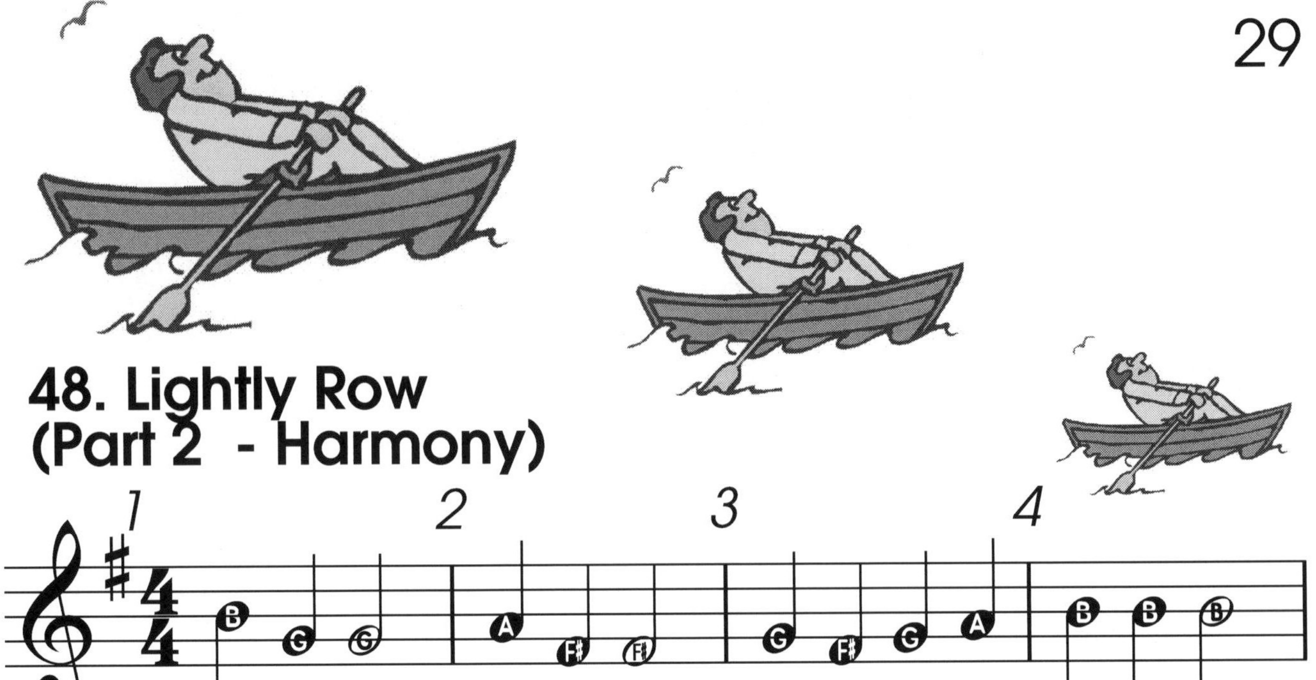

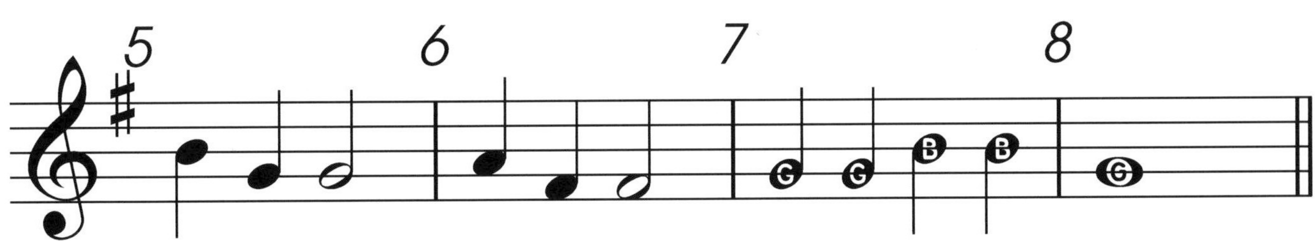

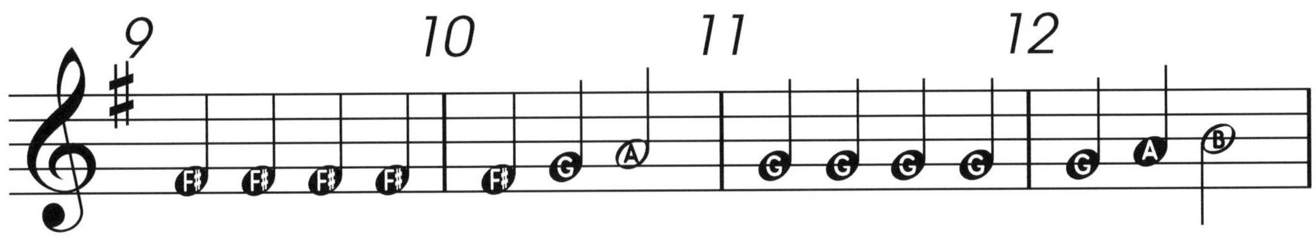

49. Good King Wenceslas

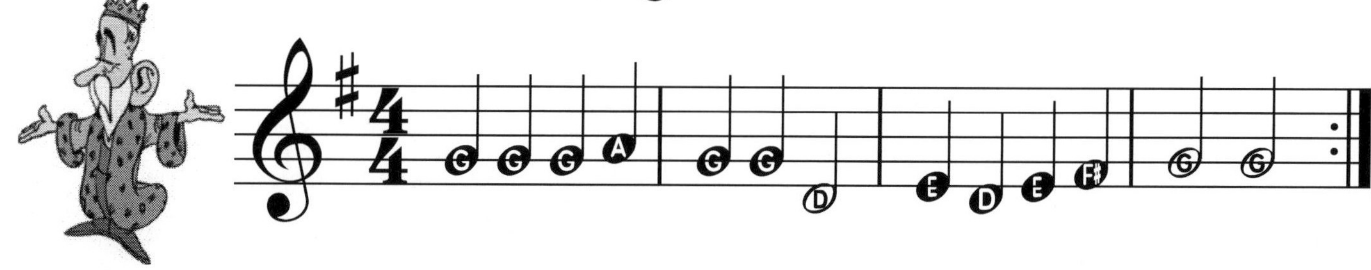

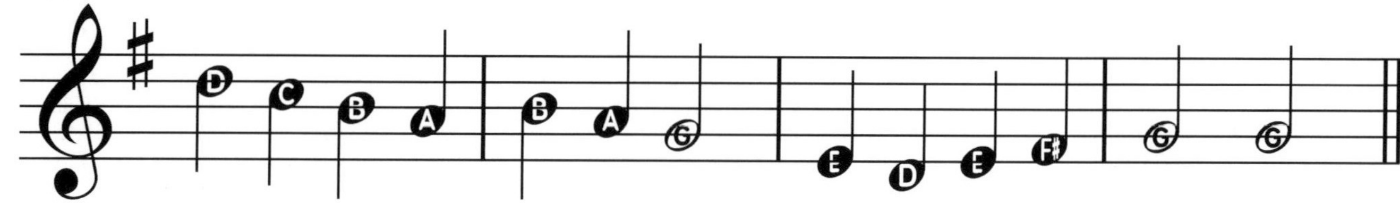

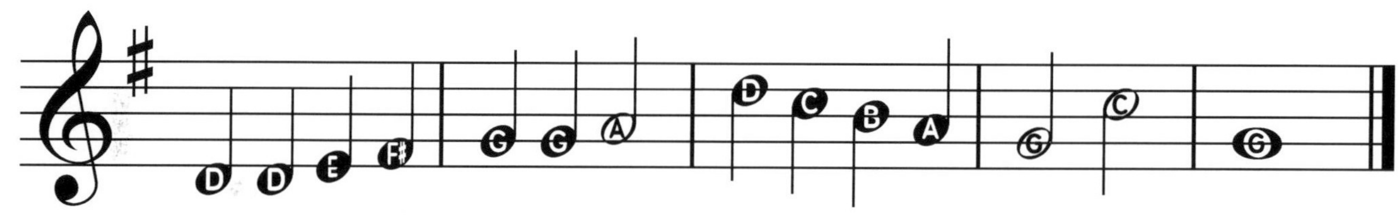

50. O Come Little Children

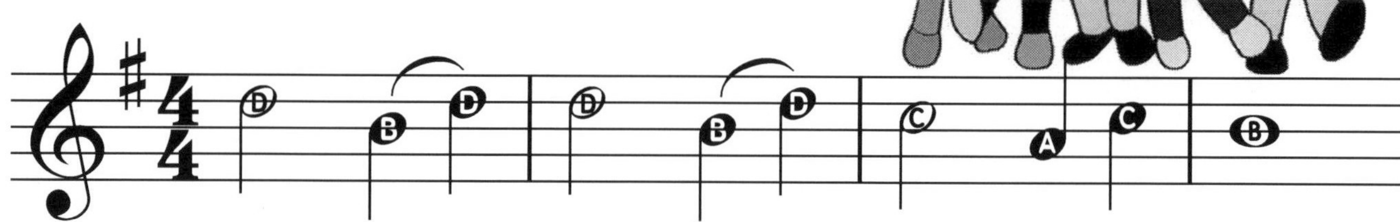

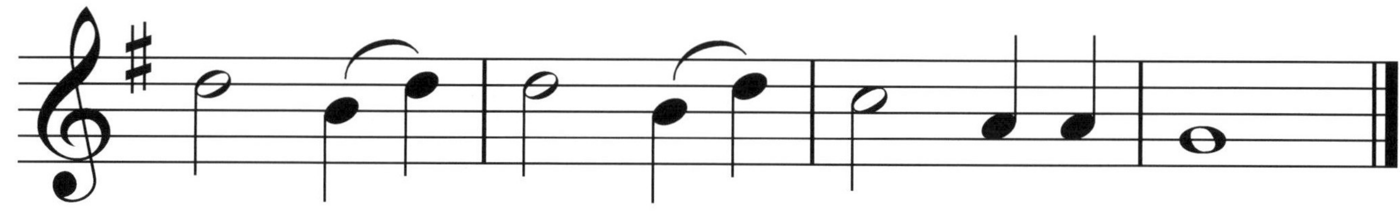

Round

Playing the same music beginning at different times.

51. Are You Sleeping?

Four Part Round

1 2 3 4

G A B G D E D C B G D

Dynamics

NEW!

p **Piano**
Play with a soft volume.

f **Forte**
Play with a full volume.

52. Minka Minka

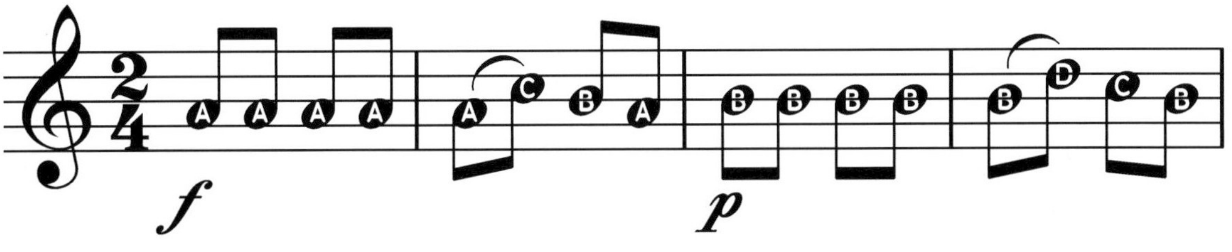

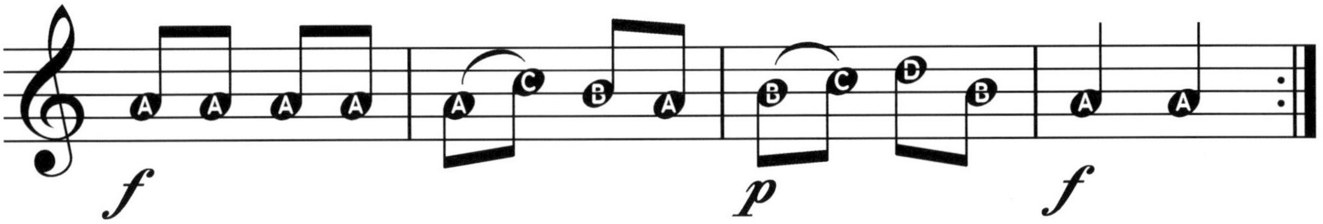

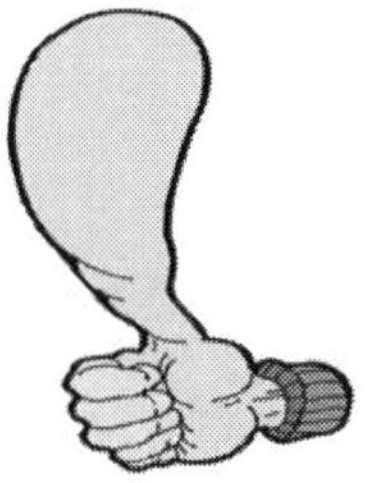

A B C D *f* *p*

53. The Thumb Slide

Dotted Quarter Note

A dotted quarter note gets one and one half counts.

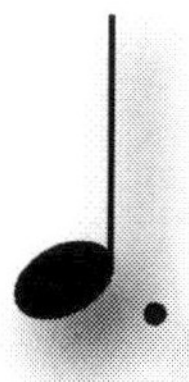

54. America

p *f* *p* *f*

www.recorderfunbook.com/page32

55. Technical Foul

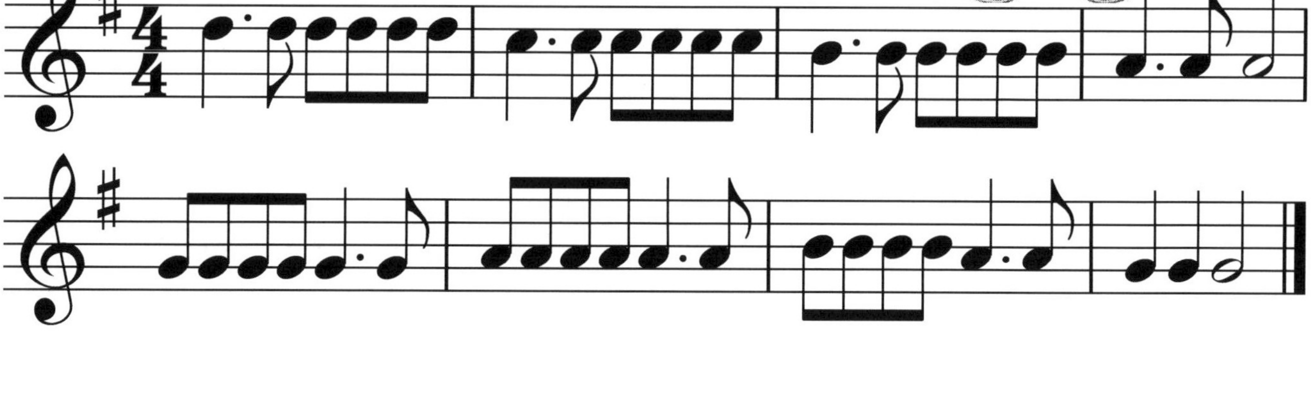

Rhythm Fun

www.recorderfunbook.com/page33

56. Rhythm Wreck
Remember to Practice!
Find time at home to practice.
Play for your parents and friends.
Perform "mini concerts."
Have fun with the recorder!
57. More Hot Cross Buns
E
D
C

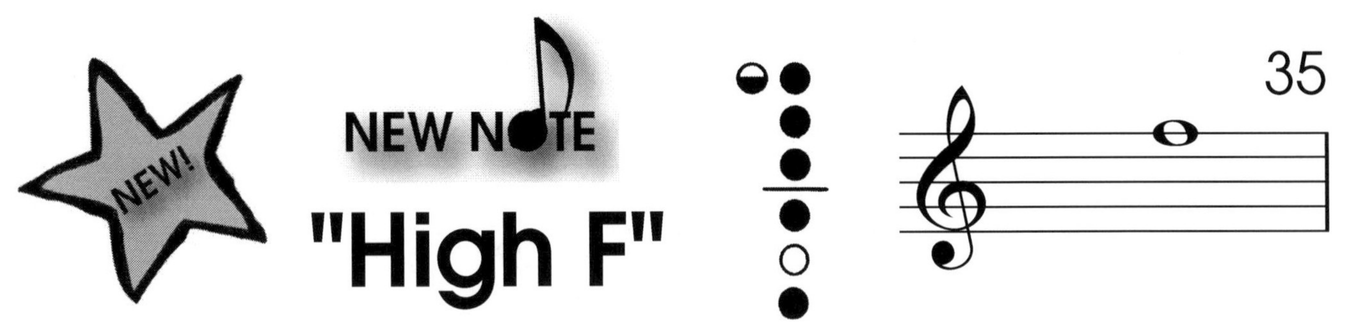

58. Hatikvah

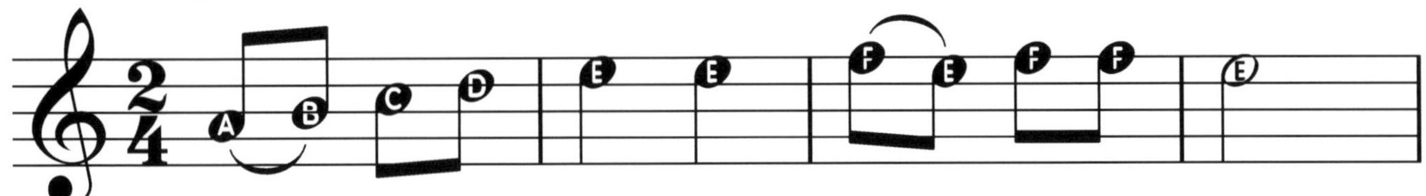

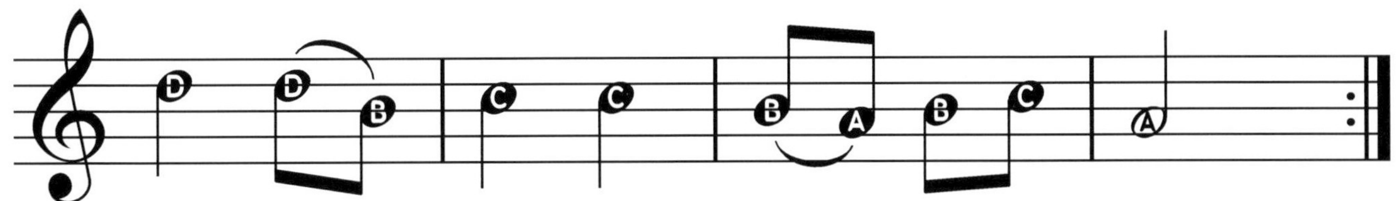

www.recorderfunbook.com/page35

59. Slippery Slurs

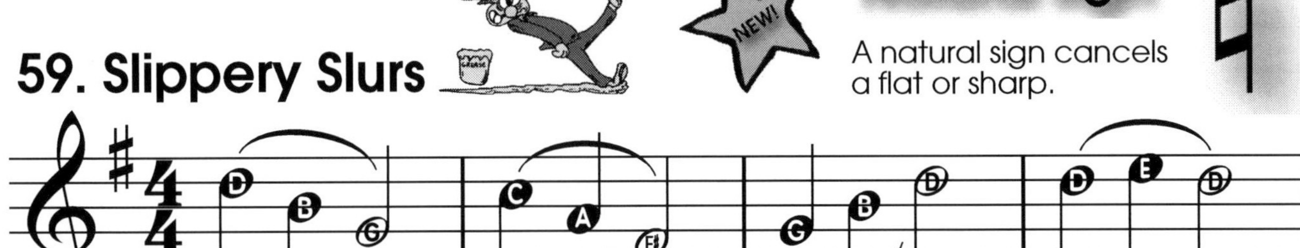

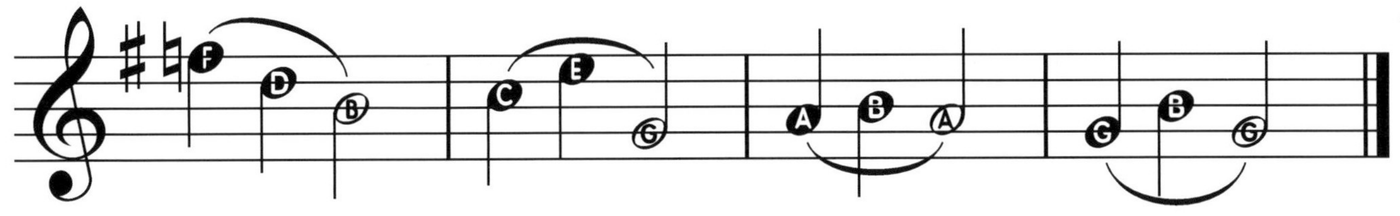

60. Bach Minuet
61. Reuben and Rachel
62. When Love Is Kind

Dynamics

NEW!

mp **Mezzo Piano**
Play with a medium soft volume.

mf **Mezzo Forte**
Play with a medium loud volume.

63. Mexican Hat Dance

64. Blues Dude

Natural Sign
A natural sign cancels a flat or sharp.

65. Big Breath Slurs

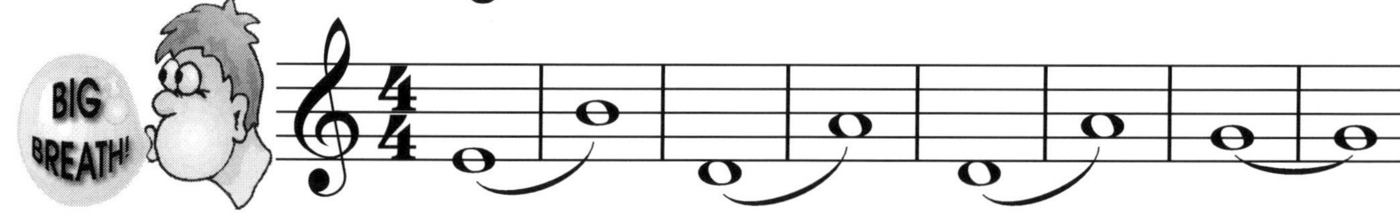

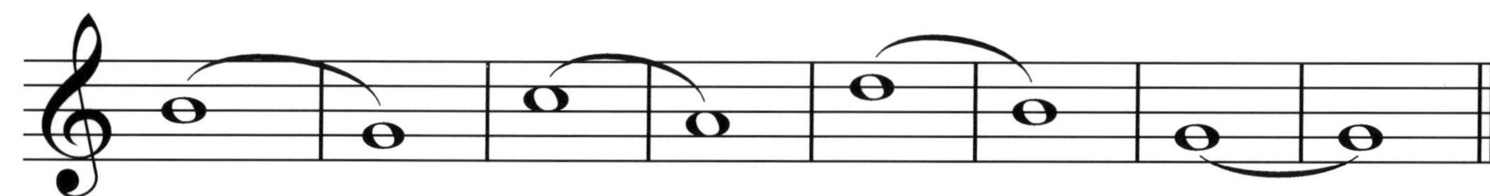

66. When the Saints Go Marchin' In

mf

mp

mf

67. William Tell Overture

68. This Old Man

69. Sweetly Sings the Donkey

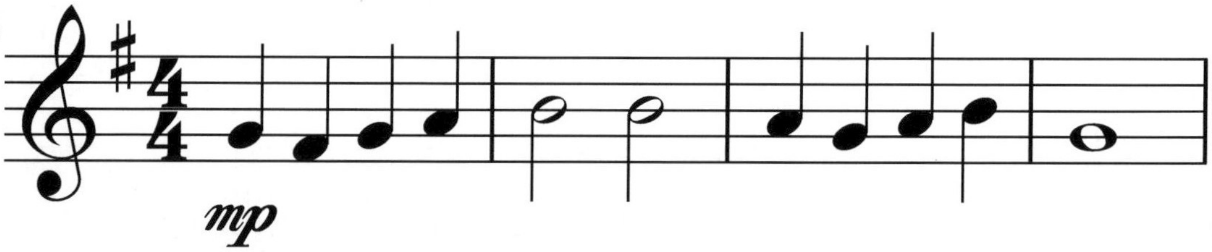

mp

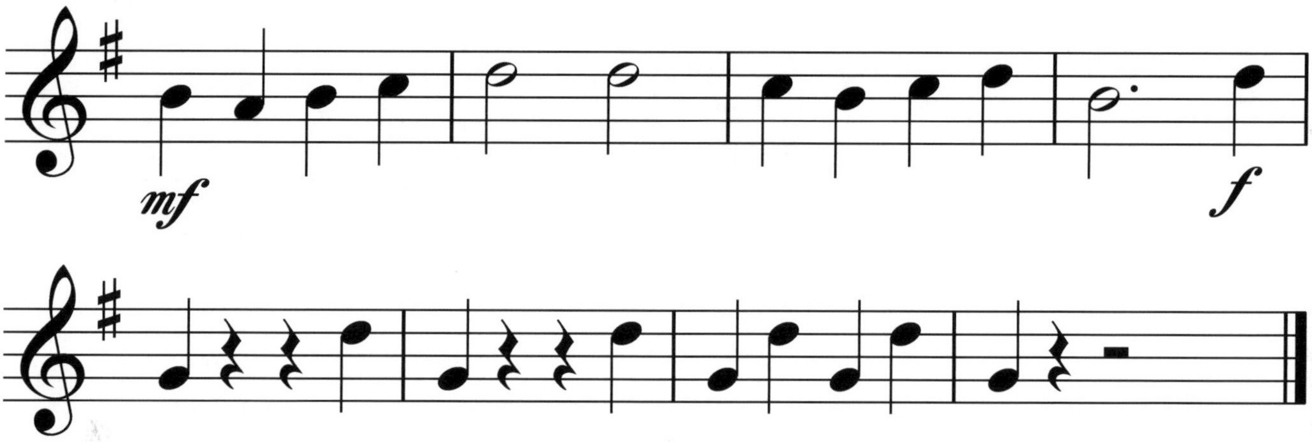

mf

f

www.recorderfunbook.com/page40

DANGER
HIGH
VOLTAGE

70. Danger! Tricky Rhythms

71. Bye, Baby Bunting

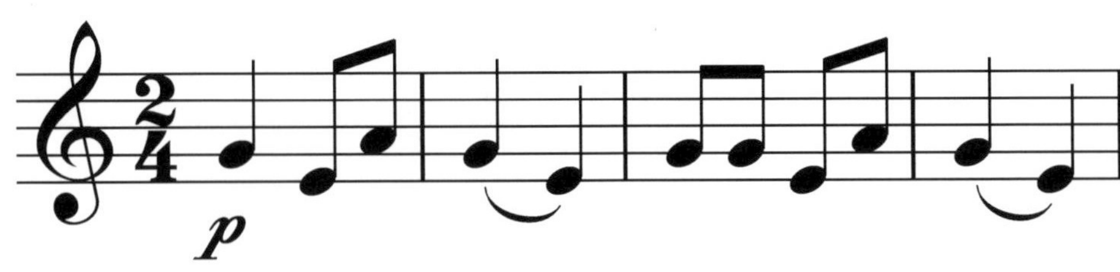

Crescendo

Get louder

Decrescendo

Get softer

72. Monster Melodies

73. Old Brass Wagon

mf

74. Kookaburra

mf

mp

75. Shortnin' Bread

76. The Erie Canal

77. Can Can
mf
1.
2.
78. La Bamba
mf

79. Simple Gifts
mp
mf
GRACE
80. Amazing Grace
mp
mf

GLOSSARY OF MUSICAL TERMS

QUARTER REST	𝄽 = One beat of silence
HALF REST	𝄼 = Two beats of silence
WHOLE REST	𝄻 = Four beats of silence

WHOLE NOTE	𝅝 = Four beats of sound
DOTTED HALF NOTE	𝅗𝅥. = Three beats of sound
HALF NOTE	𝅗𝅥 = Two beats of sound
DOTTED QUARTER NOTE	♩. = One and one half beats of sound
QUARTER NOTE	♩ = One beat of sound
Two EIGHTH NOTES	♫ = One beat of time (two sounds)
One EIGHTH NOTE	♪ = One half beat of sound

STAFF	Lines & spaces
MEASURE	Box for notes

TREBLE CLEF SIGN	𝄞 = A musical sign, found at the beginning of the staff which tells us that the notes are for the recorder and other high sounding instruments.
REPEAT SIGN	:‖ = Play the music again
DOT	• = A dot after a note adds half the value of the note.
PICK-UP NOTES	 Note(s) that come before the first full measure of a piece of music.

TIME SIGNATURE

The top number tells you how many beats in each measure.

4/4 or C	= Four beats per measure
3/4	= Three beats per measure

KEY SIGNATURE	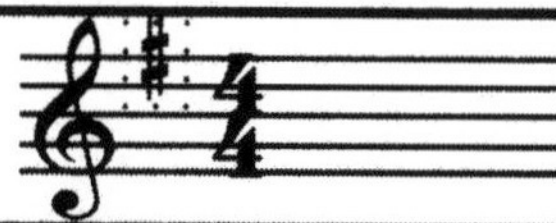	When you see one sharp at the beginning of a piece, play all the F's as F SHARP.
SHARP	 =	Raises a note one half step
ROUND		A round is played by a group. Everyone plays the same tune, but a few bars apart. The parts blend together.
FIRST & SECOND ENDINGS	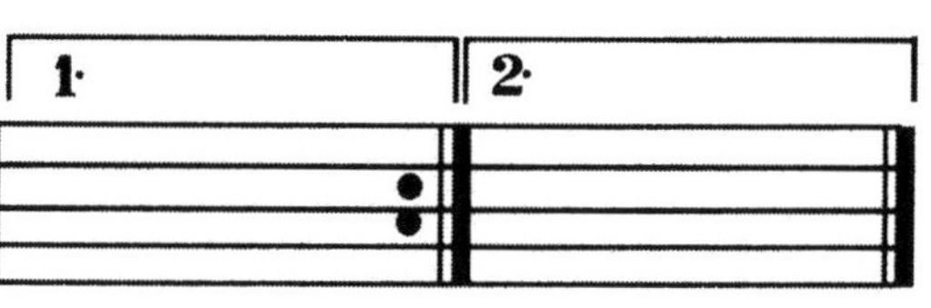 1. 2.	The first time through the piece, play the first ending and repeat as usual. The second time through, skip the first ending and play the second ending.
SLUR	 =	A **slur** is a curved line that connects two notes of different pitches. Tongue the first note and move to the second note without tonguing. Don't stop blowing.
TIE	 =	A **tie** is a curved line that connects two notes of the same pitch. Hold the note for the combined value of the two notes.
FERMATA	 =	Hold the note until your director tells you to stop.
DYNAMICS	*f* = *p* =	forte • Play with a **full** volume. piano • Play with a **soft** volume.

Recorder Fun Book Award

Congratulations on completing the Recorder Fun Book!

Signed by the Music Teacher *Date*

Bonus Coloring Pages

V is for Violin

Violin

Violin

Cello

Bass

Flute

saxophone

Trumpet

French Horn

Trombone

Tuba

Congos

Guitar

Piano

Bonus Tunes

These additional recorder tunes are available in:
The Big Song Book
Book of Easy Duets for the Recorder
and
Fifty Famous Classical Themes for Recorder

All books are available from
www.musicfunbooks.com

Chester

Chester

Haydn's Waltz

Haydn's Waltz

Latin Dancers

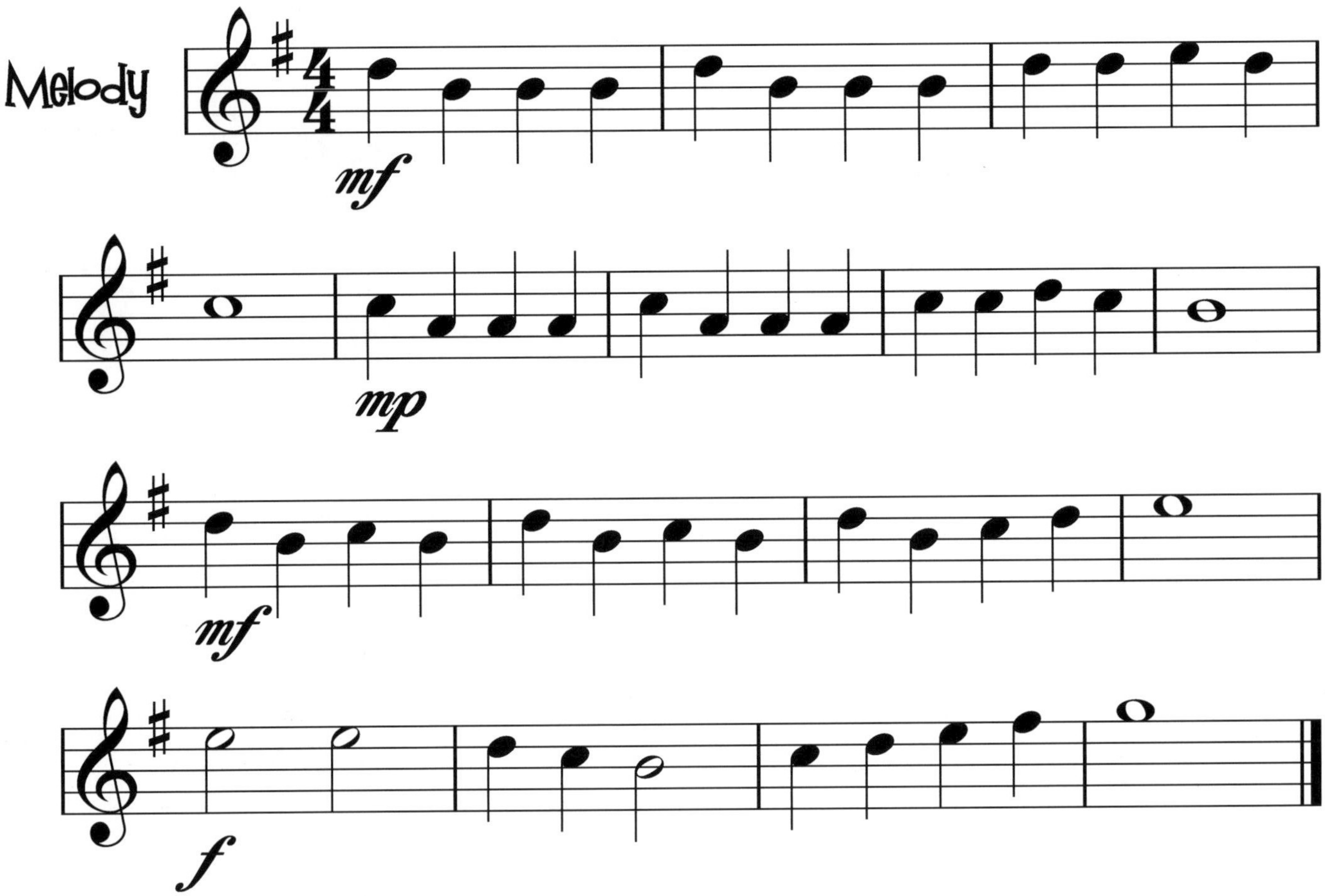
Melody
mf
mp
mf
f

See, the Conquering Hero Comes

Melody
f

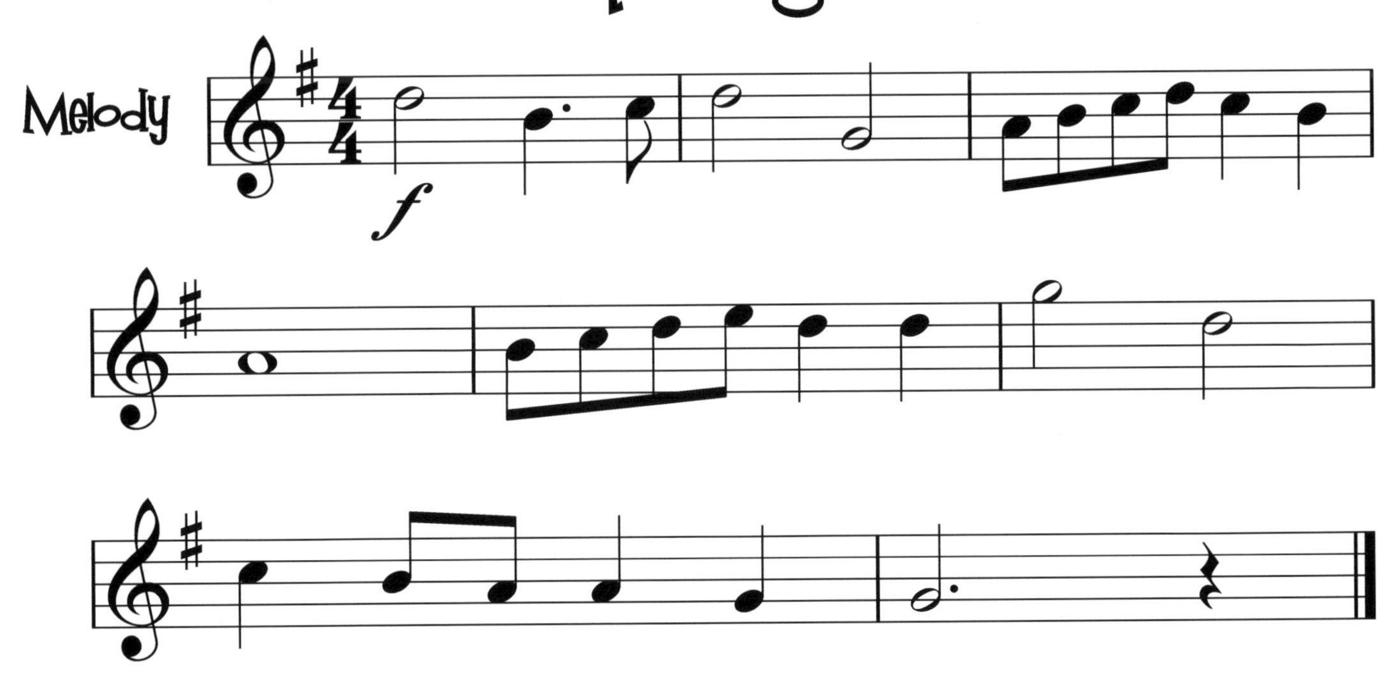

Latin Dancers

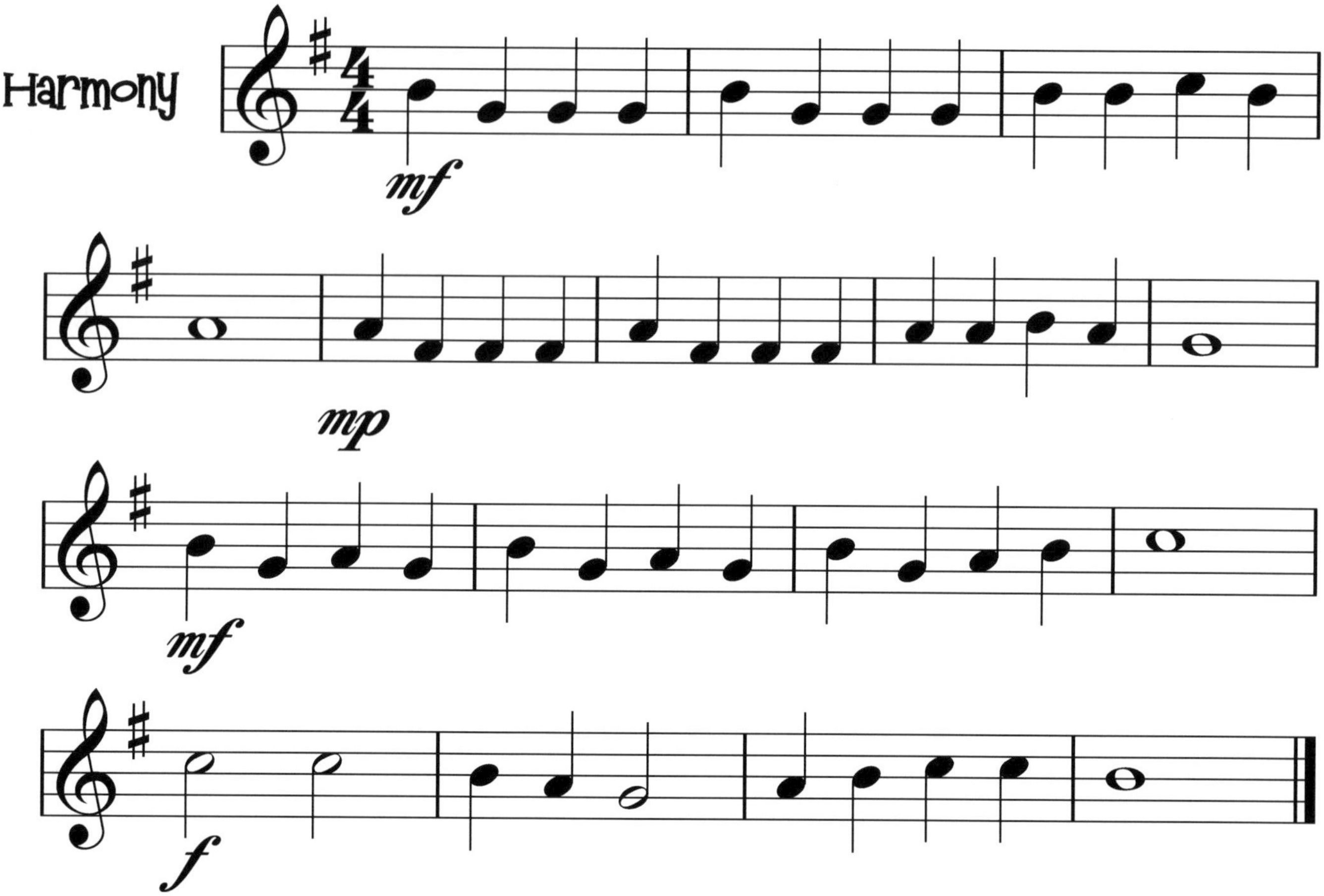
Harmony
mf
mp
mf
f

See, the Conquering Hero Comes

Harmony
f

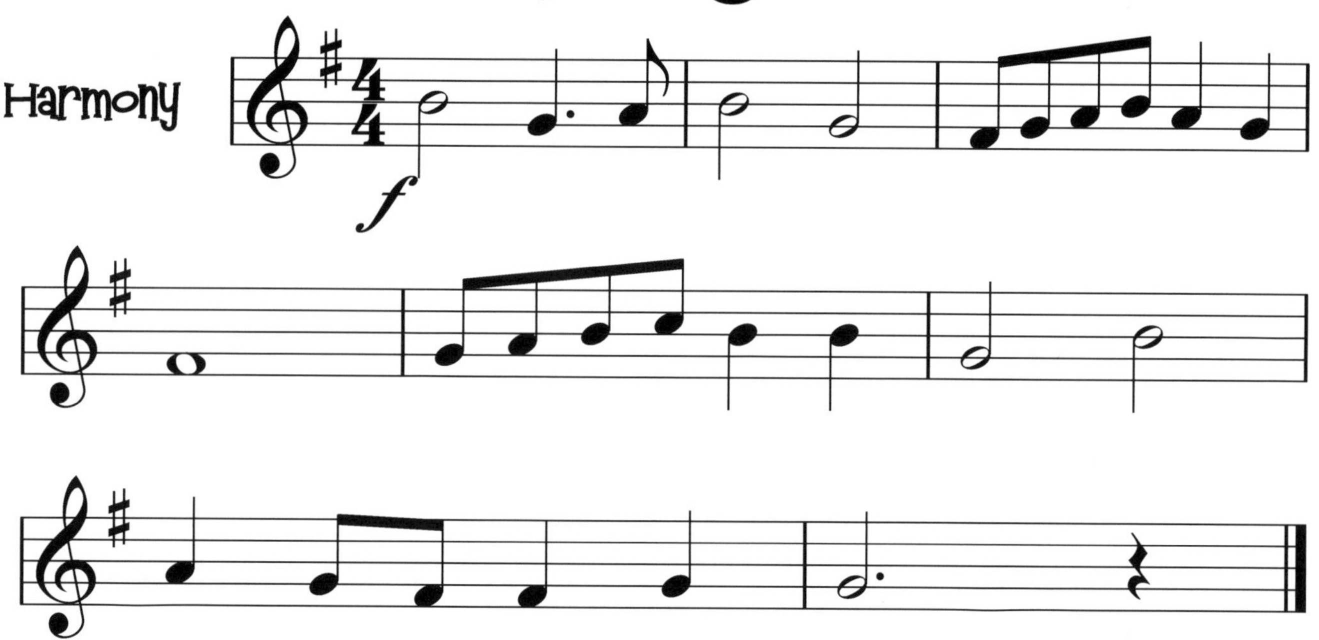

Skater's Waltz

Melody

mf

French Clowns

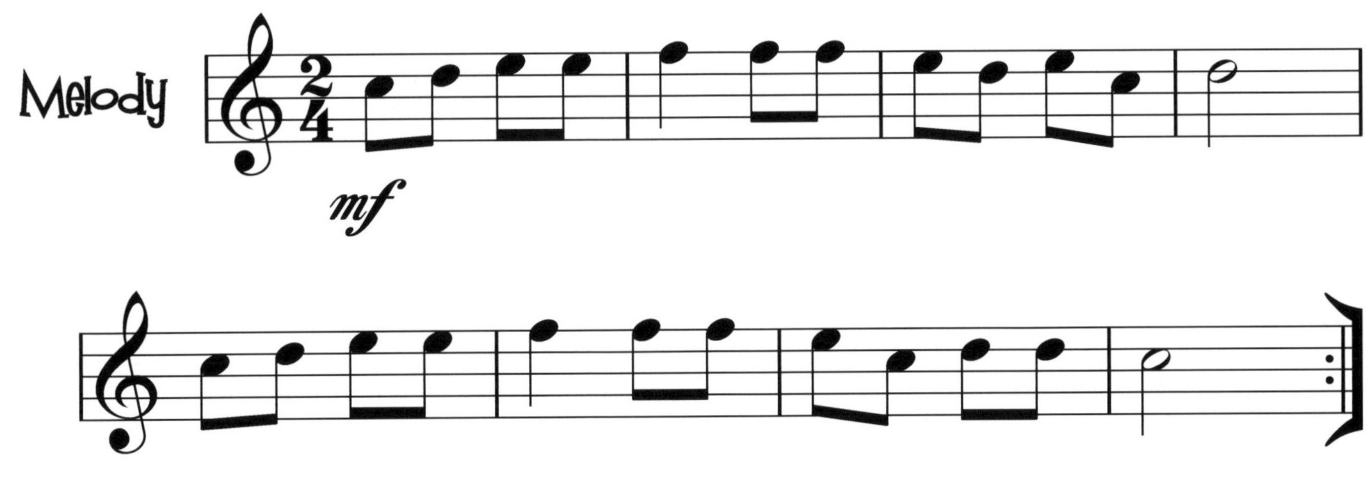

Skater's Waltz

Harmony

mf

French Clowns

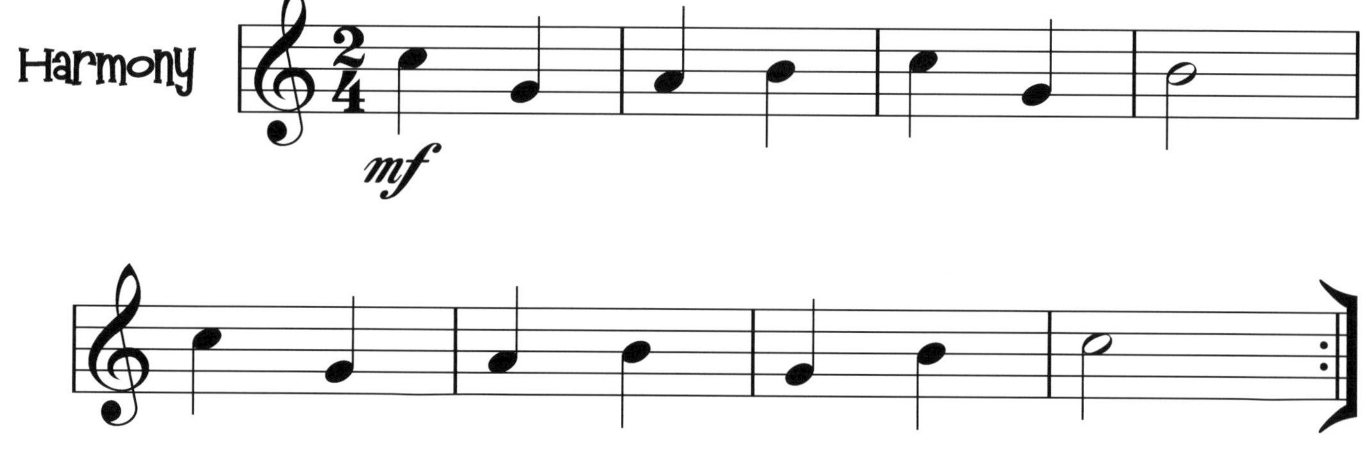

Haydn's Anthem

Haydn's Anthem

Trumpet Voluntary
Melody
mf
f
Chorale
Melody
mp

Trumpet Voluntary

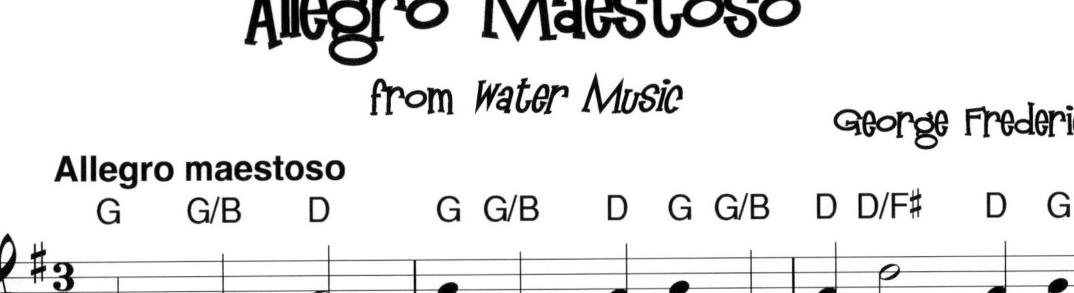
Allegro Maestoso
from Water Music
George Frederic Handel
Allegro maestoso
G G/B D G G/B D G G/B D D/F♯ D G G/B

4
D D/F♯ D G G/B D Bm/D Bm Bm/D Em Am/C Am Am/C

7
D G G/B G G/B C Am/C Am Am/C D G

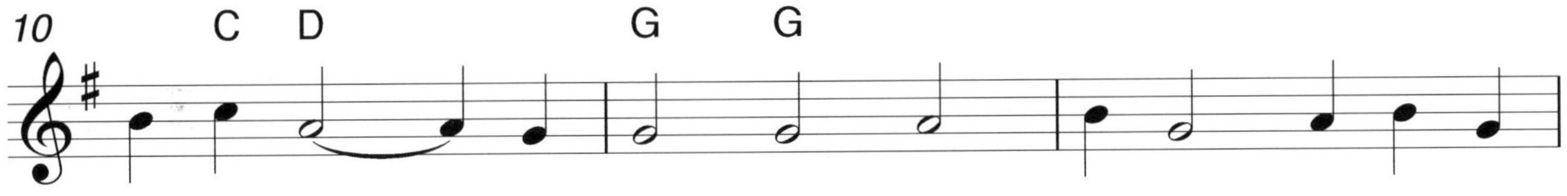
10
C D G G

13

16
Bm/D Bm Bm/D

19
Em
Am/C Am Am/C
D
G
22
Em/G Em Em/G
A
D/A D/F♯ D D/F♯
G
25
A/G
D/F♯
G
D/A
A
D
28
31
Bm/D Bm Bm/D
Em
Am/C Am Am/C
D
Em
34
Am/C
D
G
Bm/D Bm Bm/D
Em
Am/C Am Am/C
37
D
Em
Am/C
D
G

Rondeau

Jean-Joseph Mouret

A Mighty Fortress Is Our God

Finlandia

Jean Sibelius

Moderately

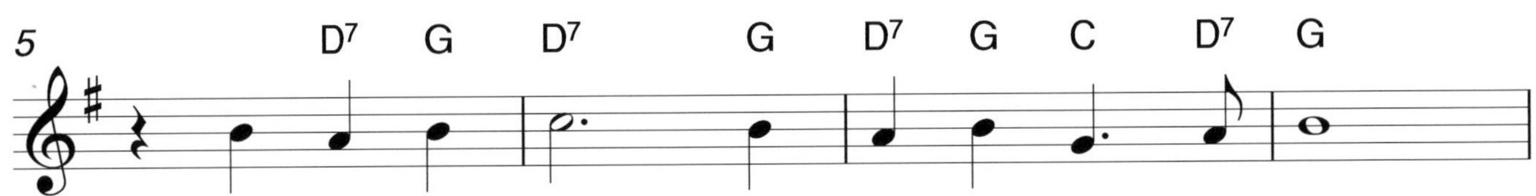

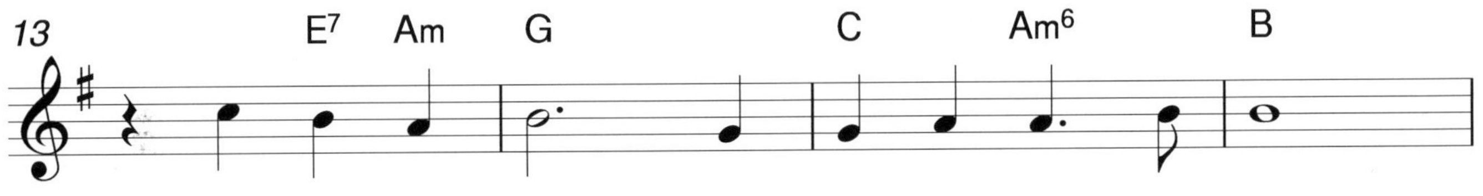

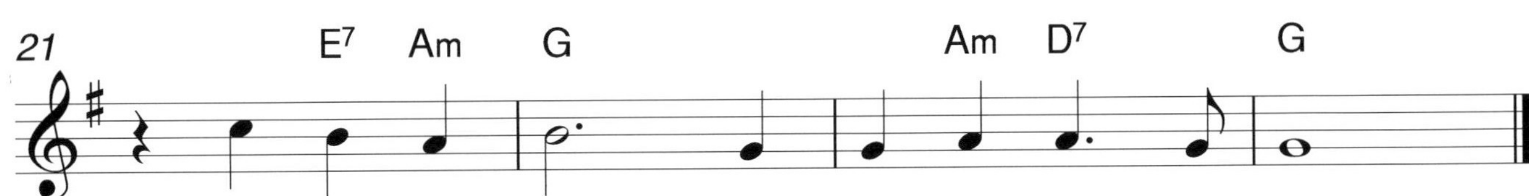

Eine Kleine Nachtmusik

K. 525, First Movement Theme

Wolfgang Amadeus Mozart

Allegro

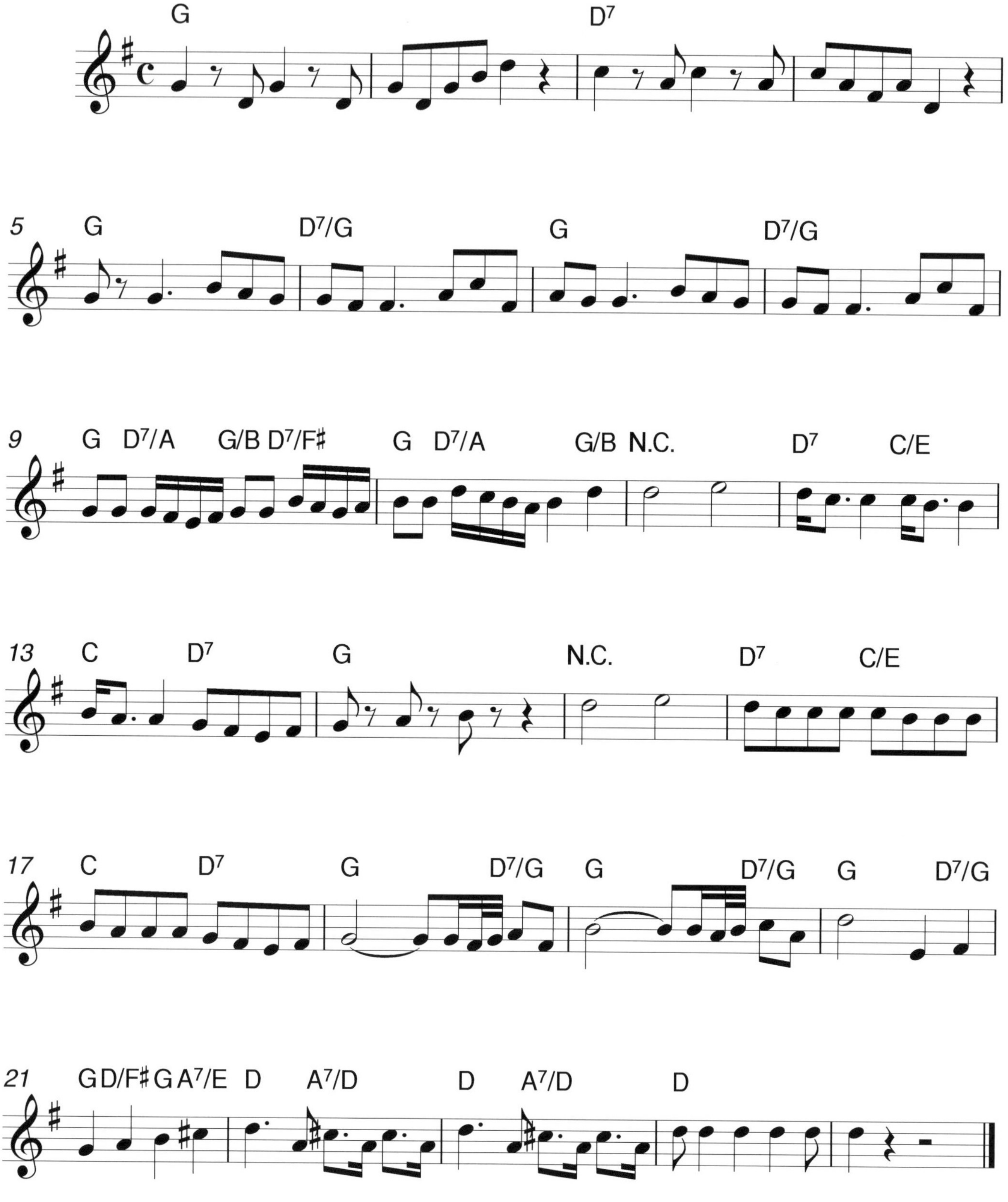
G D7
5 G D7/G G D7/G
9 G D7/A G/B D7/F♯ G D7/A G/B N.C. D7 C/E
13 C D7 G N.C. D7 C/E
17 C D7 G D7/G G D7/G G D7/G
21 G D/F♯ G A7/E D A7/D D A7/D D

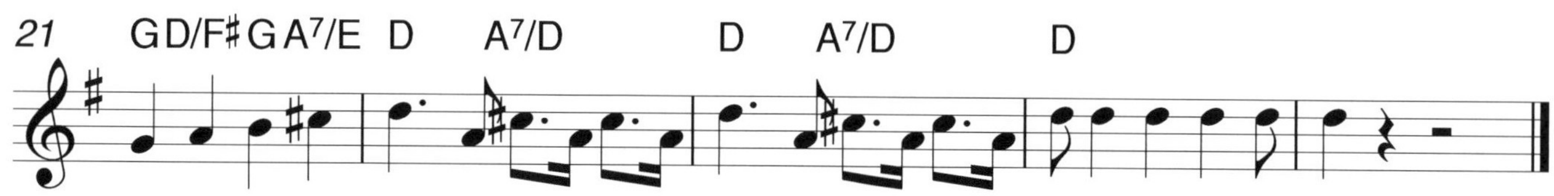

Come Again, sweet Love

John Dowland

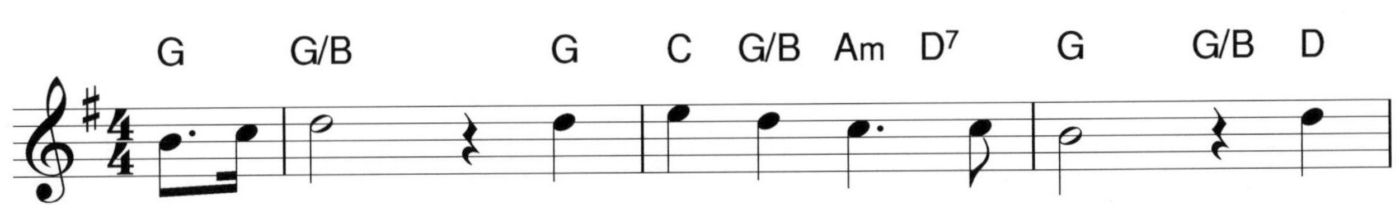

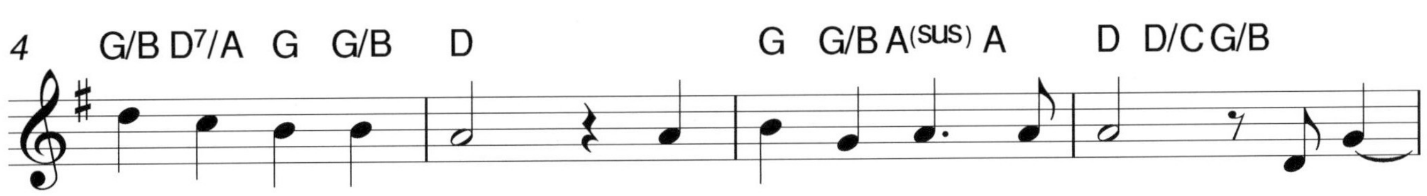

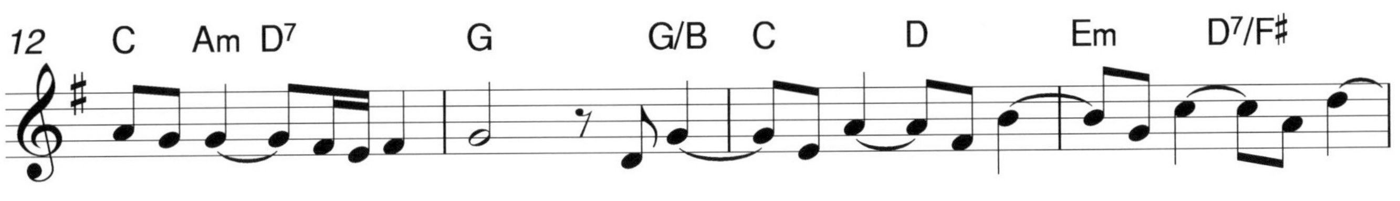

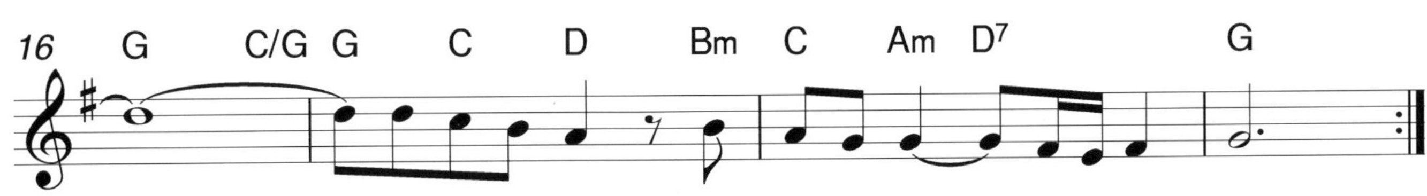

Recorder Fingering Chart • www.musicfunbooks.com

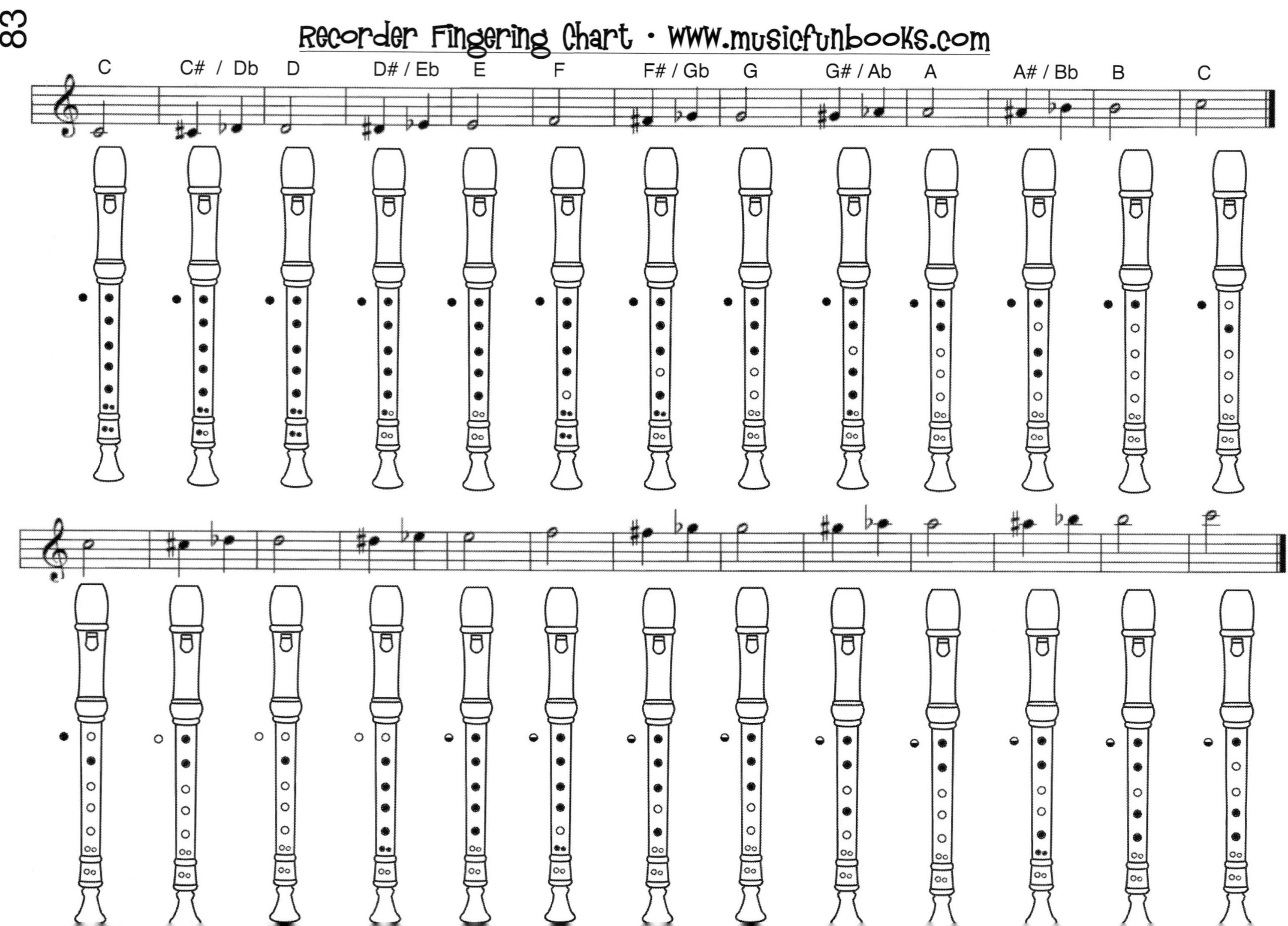

Made in the USA
Las Vegas, NV
06 September 2021